MODERN LITERARY
PERSPECTIVISM

Charles I. Glicksberg

SOUTHERN METHODIST UNIVERSITY PRESS / DALLAS

to Dorothy

CONTENTS

Modern Literary Perspectivism

INTRODUCTION

> *It is wrong to believe that historical relativism makes us incapable of evaluating and judging the work of art, that it leads to arbitrary eclecticism, and that we need, for judgment, fixed and absolute categories.*
>
> —ERICH AUERBACH

1. THE RELATIVISTIC POINT OF VIEW

THE WORD *perspectivism* in the title would seem offhand to be a culpably loose term. All-embracing in its semantic sweep, it can be made to "prove" anything the critic pleases about the work of imagination on which it is brought to bear. The only justification for it is that it constitutes in itself a point of view that makes possible a legitimate and fruitful study in aesthetics. Though tradition is a potent and enduring force in literature (Shaw is not superior to Shakespeare, as he half-seriously and half-facetiously maintained, simply because he is the beneficiary of the progress achieved during the centuries that separate them), the concept of reality changes slowly but steadily with each shift in cultural perspective. The interpretation of the world, of "the natural" and the human, of self and society, undergoes modification, sometimes almost imperceptibly but sometimes, as in the second half of the nineteenth century and the first half of the twentieth, with vertiginous speed. The point of view[1] from which a man regards the universe necessarily affects his estimate of himself and his place on earth, and all this, whether or not he is aware of it, is profoundly influ-

3

enced by the modern theory of relativity. Perspectivism, another name I shall use in this book for relativism, rests on the assumption that if the universe is mysterious and perhaps unknowable, it is quite possible in literature to portray the complex of "reality" from a seemingly inexhaustible number of points of view.

Therein clearly lies the danger of such a project as this: there is literally no end to it. If there is no limit to the number of perspectives that the writer can, theoretically, employ (and, like Dostoevski, he frequently utilizes a variety of contrasting perspectives in a dialectic of opposition), it still remains true that he cannot produce a work of art without reducing the plethoric welter of impressions to some principle of ordered unity. His sensibility cannot be allowed to run off, pell-mell, in all directions. Form must conquer the chaos of feeling. He must give birth to a *uni-verse*. What is form but an acknowledgment, both "moral" and aesthetic, on the part of the writer that while life, as Henry James observed, never begins and never ends, in the world of art there must be, however experimental its structure, a beginning and a logically interrelated and satisfying end? In holding that a work of art communicates a symbolic way, however complex, of envisioning the universe, I am not saying that this is *nothing but* a form of make-believe, a series of cherished illusions, or that, if this be so, one illusion is as good as another. Some writers, as we shall see, have on occasion held precisely this view: art as a mode of compensation for sickness, art as a symbolic act of revenge against a reality that is chaotic and incomprehensible.

Then, too, there is the cogent objection—difficult to refute—that complete relativism "leads to paralyzing skepticism, to an anarchy of values, to the acceptance of the old vicious maxim: *de gustibus non est disputandum.*"[2] But is relativism, in literature proper as in literary criticism, an exercise in irresponsibility, rendering impossible the task of "correct" representation? Is the only way out, as René Wellek argues, "a carefully defined and refined absolutism"?[3] Is Eliseo Vivas justified in branding the doctrine of relativism as "not only false but pernicious"?[4]

The fact is that perspectivism does not in practice prevent the writer and his characters from committing themselves to some point of view. No one can compose a book that does not embody a particular perspective or a series of interrelated perspectives. "To speak forth honestly is to report the world as it is beheld (however precariously) in one's own perspective."[5] And this is what I mean by perspectivism. Every proposition formulated is, according to Wittgenstein, "a picture of the universe."[6] All language, indeed, implies a conception of the universe, though—as Suzanne K. Langer demonstrates in *Philosophy in a New Key*—much of experience remains beyond the reach of knowledge. There is much that we "know" which cannot be expressed formally in language, though literature, like mystical writing, seeks to suggest the sense of the numinous and the ineffable by means of symbolism and paradox. But behind every uttered sentence there is "always a background of presuppositions which defies analysis by reason of its infinitude."[7] Language, like literature, presents an image of the world; each culture builds up its own characteristic vocabulary for interpreting the universe from a given perspective, which is chosen on the ground that it is "true."

Hence the tumultuous conflict that goes on in the literary arena between the generations, between the old and the new, the realists and the mystics, the naturalists and the romanticists, the relativists and the absolutists. Some point of view is nevertheless inescapable, even if it is only the wryly disillusioned conclusion that no single point of view is valid. The assertion that there is no "truth" (and that is the foundation on which much of modern literature rests) is also a point of view. To attempt to see all and to understand all also imposes serious, if not insurmountable, limitations.

We shall take a close look at the world of man as it is viewed from a variety of literary perspectives in our time. Sometimes these literary perspectives come into conflict, as in the battle between classicism and romanticism, and it is by no means easy to reconcile them. Though the writer as a man beholds a vision of the universe that is in keeping with his temperament and his beliefs, he is capable of entertaining, frequently at the same time, a number of clashing and incompatible points of view. Though personally he may be in sympathy with one world outlook, as an artist he must endeavor to do justice to the opposition and, if the need arises, even act as the devil's advocate. He may believe that life is a kaleidoscope of illusion, a dream within a dream, and yet protest passionately against the curse of meaninglessness. He may, like Bertold Brecht, labor to produce an "epic" theater which deliberately sets out to destroy the belief that what takes place on the stage is real, and yet create dramatic effects that are genuinely poetic and that make for some degree of empathy.

In dealing with reality through the medium of language, the writer does not produce a carbon copy. His imagination is constantly at work fashioning and transforming the reality it apprehends. Every perception is at the same time an act of interpretation. Each individual character, in fiction or drama, refracts the universe of experience through his own spectrum of sensibility. His protagonist may view life as a tragedy or comedy or farce or stupendous hoax, without necessarily being consistent in his adherence to one cosmological perspective. He may pride himself on being a nihilist like Bazarov, a down-to-earth rationalist like the hero of *What Is to Be Done?*, a man who wastes no time on music, poetry, theories, generalizations. He may be "a man without qualities," like Musil's hero, who tries out different modes of being without committing himself to any one. He may, like the antihero of Donleavy's *The Ginger Man*, believe that human effort is all in vain or, like Oblomov, dream his life away in sleep and sloth. He may regard life as a purely biological phenomenon; he may, like Artzybashev's Sanine, emulate the ideal of the superman who is not fettered by foolish notions of good and evil. The creator of these fictional personages may exalt man as the son of God or rank him as a higher species of ape.

The author of fiction is today generally invisible in his creation; he remains concealed within or behind his work, presumably Olympian in his detachment, though on occasion even a naturalist like Dreiser cannot resist the temptation to interject an auctorial comment. But the degree to which the writer maintains an attitude of godlike objectivity makes little difference in the effect his work finally produces; Hemingway, for example, is as much present in his stories and novels as Dickens and Thackeray, with their full use of author omniscience, are in theirs. The author is himself a character, however invisible or disguised, in the body of action he is bringing to life; by hewing consistently to a given point of view, he seeks to achieve a more convincing illusion of reality. Though he orchestrates the diversity of viewpoints contained in his art, he himself embodies a point of view, even if he is a Gide experimenting with the structure of the novel in *The Counterfeiters*.

In this volume I shall examine some of the different angles of vision through which writers in our time view the world. What do they take for granted, against what do they revolt, what ideal of commitment (since a choice must be made) do they seem to recommend, how do they justify their art? Whether they are in harmony with or in opposition to the dominant values of their age, they cannot help being influenced by the pressures of society and history. The historical and cultural critic is of course right, up to a point, in insisting that literature does not arise in a vacuum but grows out of its particular time-bound cultural matrix.[8] Though some of the preferred perspectives in the corpus of modern literature have clearly been influenced by the course of historical events—two world wars, communism, mechanization, the dominance of science, the use of atomic bombs, for example—the sociological approach cannot account for the emergence of "genius" or the metaphysical orientation of writers like Kafka, Andreyev, Genet, or Robinson Jeffers. For this reason, I have not considered it necessary to adhere in this book to any strict principle of chronology.

Sociologists have, to be sure, made us aware of the rich diversity of the ideological perspectives that flourish at a given time. But the writer is faced with a creative problem that transcends the sociological sphere. Whichever perspectives he brings into focus, his efforts to comprehend all of reality—and that is the nature of his Faustian ambition—are bound to fail. Inevitably his work, though psychically broadened by means of different personae, betrays its limitations. Marxist critics ingeniously "unmask" the class character of writers like Shakespeare, Ibsen, and Proust who are supposedly universal in outlook, but they do not stop to consider that literary Marxism, too, constitutes an ideology.[9]

What the novelist or dramatist comes to grips with is something more elusive and vastly more complex than the formulation of an ideology, as we find it stated, for instance, in the *Communist Manifesto* of 1848. Confronting the irreducible paradox of the human condition, the imaginative writer raises a number of questions and attempts, like the author of the book of Job, to give an "answer." His answer, however, is invariably instinct with ambiguity. What is reality? What is the self? What is the destiny of man? For what conceivable purpose was he placed on earth? The writer who believes the universe was created and ordered by God will behold a reality that is radically different from the one that the Marquis de Sade, for instance, beheld. Marlowe celebrates the advent of the self-sufficient, Faustian hero. Post-Darwinian man, convinced of the scientific truth of the doctrine of evolution, no longer argues vehemently about his animal origins or postulates a dualism between mind and body. In the case of Virginia Woolf, a character is revealed by the play of his own consciousness, so that subjective impressions afford a clue to the interior reality. Reality becomes as various as the subjectivities that react to it. Beckett, like Sartre, carries forward the epistemological debate until it culminates in a reductio ad absurdum. Perspectives meet in head-on collision. Who makes the observation that the world is an epiphenomenon, who is this observer, who thinks the thought, who utters the cry, who writes the book?

Thus it follows that what a man conceives himself to be shapes, in large measure, his interpretation of reality. Psychology is cosmology, but by the same token man's conception of the universe inevitably affects the way in which he interprets his character and destiny. Goethe's *Faust* still affirms the ideal of purposeful striving; the goal to be pursued is that of the full perfection of all one's powers on earth. It is this faith that has been challenged and overthrown by post-Goethean man. The twentieth-century Faust discerns no trace of teleology in the order or disorder of the universe. Science has deprived him of the old comforting anthropomorphic illusions. The gates of the kingdom of eternity have closed upon him, and he must live henceforth within the finite and ephemeral realm of history. He is a relativist in his perception that no system of thought is binding, no point of view privileged.

The virtue of literary perspectivism, whatever shortcomings it may have, is that it makes clear how in a work of art one image is balanced or complemented by another. Art, like the esemplastic imagination that Coleridge described, fuses elements that are opposed and seemingly irreconcilable. For the modern writer who does not believe in God, history is the court of last resort, but its decrees are equivocal and its conclusions not to be foreseen. Einsteinian physics, non-Euclidian geometry, geophysics, technological inventions, biology, the computer revolution, all of them picture a universe that is in ceaseless flux. It is impossible, henceforth, to contemplate the human scene *sub specie aeternitatis*. The modern writer, as Sartre emphasizes, must consequently abandon his idea of imposing a privileged point of view on his creation. He must present

creatures whose reality would be the tangled and contradictory tissue of each one's evaluations of all the other characters—himself included—and the evaluation by all the others of himself, and who could never decide from within whether the changes of their destinies came from their own efforts, from their own faults, or from the course of the universe.[10]

Presumably the reader, too, would be denied a privileged position. Thus we get a conception of destiny, characteristically modern, that can be interpreted in a variety of ways, none of which is right and all of which may be wrong. Perspectivism in literature today provides a version of existence that is ambiguous and enigmatic.

As I have said, literary perspectivism cannot possibly succeed in reporting every point of view that the eye of the mind can behold; it assumes that each angle of vision is relative. And this holds true even when the writer, like John Dos Passos in *U.S.A.*, employs a series of shifting points of view, including the newsreel technique, the camera eye, and biographical capsule studies of important men in the time covered by the story. To realize that this is so makes for a skepticism that is humble rather than arrogant, liberating rather than paralyzing. The perception born of relativism drives home the lesson of the insuperable limitations of art as well as knowledge. Impossible of attainment is the aim of a novelist like Thomas Wolfe to include everything within the compass of his vision. André Gide ruefully confesses in *The Counterfeiters* that "it would probably be foolish to collect into a single novel everything life offers me and teaches me. However closely packed I want this book to be, I cannot hope to get everything in. And yet this desire still bothers me."[11]

This is the conflict the modern writer is involved in: he strains for all-inclusiveness but is held back by the refractoriness of his medium, the limitations of language and of art. Not that he consciously functions like a perspectivist, even when, like Gide, he breaks up the stream of action by commenting upon his creative difficulties as he composes the novel. He may wrestle with all sorts of technical and metaphysical questions, but he must, in the last analysis, abide by the truth of his feelings and insight. Since he is not God (though he may usurp the role), he must perforce report what is true for him; he makes the effort, however, to record what is true for others who are differently constituted and who are placed in circumstances unlike his own. Whatever he does, he cannot capture the whole universe of experience. The nature of reality baffles the most nobly endowed imagination.

2. PERSPECTIVISM AND REALITY

Up until the nineteenth century, the writer confronted a universe that seemed rational and ordered; at least he thought it made sense. The Newtonian system was a perfect illustration of cosmic harmony. In the twentieth century, however, as the doctrine of relativity has gained the ascendancy, nature is seen as process not substance, as flux not fixity. Reality is infinitely protean in its manifestations. The scientific revolution has wrought havoc with the absolutes of the past.

But perspectivism did not emerge suddenly as a new literary discovery in the twentieth century. It has its roots and antecedents in the past. But it differed sharply, in degree if not in kind, from the perspectives used by such writers as Cervantes, Rabelais, Montaigne, and Shakespeare.[12] Cervantes is essentially modern in his handling of the perspectivism that informs *The Adventures of Don Quixote* as a whole.[13] He is aware that the world can be interpreted in a variety of ways; each of his characters reacts differently to his environment, while Cervantes observes the action of the plot from his own privileged position as author. Cervantes displays remarkable ingenuity in revealing the face of reality not as it is (there is, despite Kant, no such thing-in-itself), but as it is refracted through the sensibility of his principal dramatis personae. And yet, writing as he did in an age in Spain when Catholicism was still unchallenged, he never himself questions the reality of the supernatural.[14]

The battle between relativists and absolutists has thus been going on for some time, though the absolutists had it their own way until late in the seventeenth century. It was in the middle of the eighteenth century that dissent became articulate and formidable. Not until then "was there any conscious and systematic attempt to apply the relativistic approach to literary evaluation."[15] What happened to make modern perspectivism distinctive was the result in part of Einstein's work in revolutionizing the Newtonian model of a universe bound by space and time and in part the result of a new approach to the conception of time provided by psychoanalysis.[16] What we get in modern literature is the triumph of psychological perspectivism. As Koestler points out, "The relativity of psychological time has nothing to do with the relativity of time in physics."[17]

Reality, thus relativized, is transformed into a construct of emergent relationships, forever changing in accordance with the point of view of the observer. There are no established facts, no predetermined objects, no solid and enduring forms. No thing is simply there, frozen in that position for all of time. As the philosophy of permanence is jettisoned, reality takes on a bewildering multiplicity of aspects; it is both one and many, a fusion of opposites. The principle of polarity comes into operation, so that *yes* ceases to be *yes* and slides over in meaning to *no*. As D. T. Suzuki says, "There is no hard and fast division between 'yes' and 'no.' It is in the nature of life that it is so."[18] Ionesco, early in his career, presented two essays, side by side, "under the title of *No!*, to prove the possibility of holding opposite views on the same subject, and the identity of contraries."[19] The world is not only an enigma but a Dionysian dance of electrons, an arena of contending forces.

Reality inevitably assumes a different configuration of meaning as it is seen from different points of view in the time-space continuum. In vain does Wyndham Lewis release his impassioned polemic, *Time and Western Man*, to defend the solid, substantial world of space against the disintegrating flux of the philosophers of the time cult like Alexander, Whitehead, Bergson, and Bertrand Russell. If no view of the universe affords a total picture, if no system of thought can be all-embracing, then the artist is justified in portraying each of his characters as dwelling in a unique world of his own. Reality cannot be the same for all. It is open—and that is the burden of my theme—to a host of interpretations, each of which is equally authentic or perhaps equally mistaken.[20] There can be no definitive answer to the all-important question of what reality is. "Obviously," as one critic remarks, "no literary character can contain the infinite and inexhaustible wealth of features and reactions to be found in life itself."[21]

Though realism rejects the realm of subjectivity, it is rarely rigorously consistent in practice. The attempt to define realism in literature is attended with considerable semantic confusion. Literary realism, whatever form it takes, rests on a metaphysical as well as aesthetic base; it aims to present a simulacrum of reality "on the basis of more or less fixed rules."[22] It undertakes to arrive at nothing less than "the truth." The scientific method of observation and inquiry seemed to provide a reliable way of exploring new areas of experience, and Zola tried to apply it in the Rougon-Macquart series. In the twentieth century, socialist realism departs from the tenets of realism in that it believes literature should portray the revolutionary development of society. The writer is, in effect, committed to the task of supporting the cause of the proletariat; he must take sides in the social conflict, but there is only one "just" side for him to espouse. Reality must be shaped imaginatively as well as ideologically in the desired Marxist-Leninist-Stalinist direction. Consequently what we get in Soviet fiction is a form of revolutionary idealism. But in general what identifies the Marxist critic is the conviction that it is the duty of the writer to reflect "objective" social reality. Though realists differ in their methods of portrayal, they do, as Lukacs says, "inexorably depict the true essence of reality."[23] There we have it, the telltale dogmatic phrase: "the true essence of reality."

Critical realism, naturalism, socialist realism, as applied to the novel, give no indication of literary value. They merely indicate that the author has embraced a particular philosophy of nature or of society. They do, however, illustrate the point that literature can be composed and judged according to divergent perspectives. But if literature is always situated within a social frame of reference, it is also the locus of metaphysical insights and of spiritual illuminations having little to do with the temporal or social domain. The mystery remains: the ineffable privacy of the personal self as well as the intractably complex content of the "real." If literature reveals much about the conditions of society at a given time, it also reveals much more: the world of dreams, the dimensions of subjectivity, the nostalgia of the absolute, the Pascalian reasons of the heart.[24] All perception is shot through with the ubiquitous "I." It is precisely this personal perspective that constitutes the ambiguous reality of the world and that serves to shape the form of the literary experience. As Julian Marias points out: "To say 'world' is to say 'my world,' just as to say 'I' at once implies a 'world' or circumstances."[25] Man dwells in the physical world, but he is also associated with other beings; hence he lives simultaneously in three worlds: that of nature, that of society, and that of the self.

What literature does, among other things, is to portray the ambiguity of the human adventure. The writer views the strange spectacle of life through a series of provisional perspectives. Kafka suggests a reality behind the reality of the senses. In order to describe his experience of cosmic alienation and suggest the existence of that which lies beyond the range of "known" reality—namely, the absence of order or purpose so far as the mind can make out—he relied on the use of parable. The parable intimated the presence of something behind or beyond phenomena, without Kafka's ever asserting that this has any reality.[26] All literature, all language, is, like thought itself, inescapably metaphorical.[27]

3. *LITERATURE AND PHILOSOPHY*

The novelist, like the dramatist, is not a philosopher nor even a purveyor of ideologies. He creates characters who come alive through action and experience; each of his fictional personages is the bearer of a private self, but each is also part of an objective social environment which influences him for better or worse and which he, in turn, helps to transform. Most of the complexities of fiction and drama stem from this polarity of subjectivity and objectivity, dream and reality, illusion and truth. Subjectivity, like spirit, can manifest itself only by being incorporated within a body; it is revealed, however ambiguously, by a consciousness directed toward the world outside. Consciousness interprets the world of experience, just as the world shapes consciousness.

But a number of modern writers owe much to the philosophical heritage bequeathed to them by men like Schopenhauer and Nietzsche. It is Nietzsche in particular who must be hailed as a bold pioneer in the field of perspectivism. He is the philosopher of relativism *par excellence*. He emphasized the degree to which all that man beholds and believes is dependent on his point of view. The mind unavoidably interposes itself between what is there and what is seen. There is no correspondence between thought and reality. Logic discloses that reality does not rest on a foundation of logic. As for the noumenal character of reality, that can never be known. Once the absolute is scrapped, it then becomes ridiculous to assume that the perspective the mind happens to adopt is the only true one. On the contrary, says Nietzsche, the world "has once more become 'infinite' to us: in so far as we cannot dismiss the possibility that it contains infinite interpretations."[28] Glorying in a world that conformed to no rational standards of order, Nietzsche argued that the free spirit can do without the prop of certainty. Undermining the assumptions on which much of nineteenth-century literature and thought rested, he encouraged his followers to exploit the aesthetic perspective.

If the artist is today overwhelmed by the terrifying sense of being lost in the empty spaces of the infinite, he attempts, by the urge to abstraction, to tear the object out of its natural context.[29] In literature, however, this urge to abstraction cannot exorcise the specter of meaninglessness. In his early work, *The Temptation of the West*, Malraux lucidly faces the horror of the absurd. When A. D., a young Frenchman in this epistolary dialogue, complains to Ling, a young Chinese, that the shadow of the absurd always lurks in the background, the latter remarks: "For you, absolute reality was first God, then Man; but Man is dead, following God, and you search with anguish for something to which you can entrust his strange heritage."[30] What the westerners call "reality" has become progressively more alien and apparitional. And A. D. concedes that Europe is dominated by "the impossibility of grasping any reality whatever."[31] The absurd hero of the twentieth century, like Meursault in *The Stranger*, is forced to accept a universe which is incomprehensible.

This volume will undertake to examine some of the ways in which modern writers interpret the ongoing human quest for meaning. It will show that the viewer cannot eliminate himself from the act of perception. The first part will discuss in considerable detail how perspectivism functions in the context of modern literature. Then it proceeds to analyze the character of the vital metaphors and symbols that are elaborated in the work of such writers as Maeterlinck, Salvador Dali, Dostoevski, Pirandello, Hermann Hesse, Adamov, and Genet. Life as a dream, the myth of the unconscious, art as decadence and disease, life as a game that must be played according to the prescribed rules, life as a stage: these are some of the perspectives that are brought under critical scrutiny. The second part, called "Counterperspective," appraises the contribution made by such figures as Chernyshevski and Bertold Brecht and focuses attention on the perspectives they assert. In addition, it takes up the utopian obsession as set forth, positively and negatively, in the writings of H. G. Wells, Aldous Huxley, and B. F. Skinner. The last three chapters deal, respectively, with the scientific perspective, the search for a saving myth, and the gospel of Inhumanism preached by Robinson Jeffers.

The writer probes the nature of reality, but life is more complex than any literary or philosophical summing up. What he frequently attempts to do is to break down the compartmentalization of reality, to rise above the discursive concepts of science. The "laws" which govern the motion of molecules and electrons cannot be legitimately applied to the portrayal of human reality. The vision of the artist and of the mystic is as "real" as that of the scientist.[32] What takes place inside the self is as "real" as what occurs in the world outside. As one psychologist eloquently maintains, "Reality," as a metaphysical counter, is "an honorific, not a descriptive, term. We call 'real' the world as viewed from our preferred orientation."[33]

PART ONE / RELATIVISM IN ACTION

1. PERSPECTIVISM AND RELATIVISM

THOUGH ATTEMPTS have been made to distinguish between the two terms, the philosophy of perspectivism is but another name for relativism. Karel Capek, in defending the idea of relativism that informs his novel *Factory for the Absolute* (1922), declares: "For me it is the only path by which it is possible to come to love for man when we have lost our faith in humanity; the only way to come to a love for the search for truth when we cannot find truth; to unite the most shameful skepticism with a naive and effectual trust."[1] It provides a stimulating and infinitely fruitful source of vision. It saves him from taking refuge in dogmatism; he is not likely to fall into the common mistake of assuming that the norms of his culture or age are universal categories of value, since he realizes that no two people live in the same time-space continuum. It makes for a chancy, wide-open universe of discourse.

Capek is nevertheless aware that while perspectivism does not culminate in a paralyzing skepticism, it does impose a heavy handicap on the man who embraces it. He must arrive at an altogether new conception of truth, nature, reality, and of course the problematical character of man himself. In such a confused and protean field of reference, nothing is certain. No fixed moral or epistemological standards can be used as a guide. *Human* reality cannot be reduced to scientifically warranted coordinates. One man's truth is another man's error. If this be a damnable conclusion to reach, it is one amply borne out today by psychological experience. What the scientist regards as empirically substantiated is considered by a thinker like Kierkegaard or an antirationalist like Unamuno to be a gross error; truth is subjectivity. Science, too, is a "myth."

But no one can long remain with any degree of spiritual comfort in a completely relativized universe. He must needs believe, if only for the brief time of his life, that his sense-data can be objectively confirmed, that existence, his in particular and that of mankind as a whole, is meaningful. Unfortunately there is no single orientation which he can accept as true, no particular world outlook which can satisfy all his needs. It is this self-defeating quest for ultimate meaning that makes up the theme of much of modern literature. The twentieth-century writer has come to a point where, like Samuel Beckett, Ionesco, and Joyce, he distrusts language—and art too—as a distorting, if not treacherous, medium: not a mirror or a lamp but a lie. Like Gide, he cannot get himself to believe that consciousness confirms "the truth" of what it beholds in the world outside; he must perforce place his trust in instinct and the testimony of the senses, though he is inclined to wonder that a world should exist at all.

In the world of the imagination, however, perspectivism is neither a drawback nor a serious danger but a challenge. The writer exploits a series of as-if fictions as a means of "universe-building." Even though the world outside fails to conform to his dreams and myths, he needs to view it from a given vantage point before he can discover that this is so, indeed, before he can venture to say anything at all. His mythopoeic faculty may envisage the life of man as a pilgrim's progress, a journey celestial or infernal, a divine comedy, a delightful dream within a dream or a frightening nightmare, a mystery that can never be solved except by an absurd "leap" of faith. Theoretically, he enjoys God's plenty in his choice of possible metaphors to embody his vision of the world and his interpretation of man. But there is a vast difference between working with fictions that are known to be fictions, myths that are frankly utilized as myths, and believing in them as true reflections of the master model, nature. In twentieth-century literature as in philosophy, fictions are accepted not because they are "true" but because of what they have to offer as vital illusions or provisional perspectives.

2. THE PHILOSOPHY OF AS-IF FICTIONS

From the beginning of his career, Hans Vaihinger, the philosopher, recognized the possibility that a fiction might be in error and yet prove fundamentally helpful. Like Nietzsche and Eduard von Hartmann, he derived from Schopenhauer his insight into the irrationalism that pervades life. The irrational enters disturbingly, though often in disguised form, into the life of nature and the course of history. Vaihinger concludes that thought, reason, knowledge are only *means* employed by the life-force to achieve its own obscure purpose. Thought, by attempting to throw off the tyranny of the will, is confronted by problems utterly beyond its power to solve. Elaborating Kant's doctrine that the finite human mind can grasp only phenomena and not noumena, he argues that man is impotent to solve the riddle of existence. In 1876 he wrote his dissertation entitled "Logical Studies Part 1: The Theory of Scientific Fictions," which is the same work published in 1911 as *The Philosophy of 'As If'*, except that he added two other parts and then a final section on Nietzsche's theory of fictions. His thesis holds "that 'As if', i.e. appearance, the consciously-false, plays an enormous part in science, in world-philosophies and in life."[2]

The implications of the fictive or relativistic method of analysis are important for aesthetics as well as for ethics and metaphysics. If ideas are designed not to mirror reality but to furnish us with instruments of adaptation, then it is not possible to eliminate the distortions induced by consciousness and subjectivity. The principle of indeterminacy comes into its own. Objects and events are interpreted *as if* they behaved in accordance with some mind-projected principle, causality for example, though there is no justification for assuming that they do. If there is no bridge from sense-data to the external world, if the two spheres of the subjective and the objective cannot be brought into harmony, then the problem of cognition is insoluble. The mind is driven to employ fictions heuristically if it is to make any sense at all of the phenomena of life. Actually, as Vaihinger asserts, it is foolish "to question the meaning of the universe."[3] Consciousness does not simply reflect objects outside it; it shapes and colors the reality it apprehends. Since reality can never be known objectively, what thought does is to elaborate sense-data into a number of concepts or metaphors so that events in the world can be predicted. Hence the urgent necessity for relying on fictions if the organism is to relate itself effectively to the world it lives in. "The history of mankind is full of examples proving the existence not only of fruitful errors . . . but also of *harmful truths*."[4]

This, then, is the challenging thesis Vaihinger propounds: ideas, concepts, values, and beliefs are produced by the mind without much regard for their empirical validity; they are purely fictional constructs, the aim of which is somehow to make sense of the booming, buzzing confusion of the phenomenal flux. Thought and reality do not correspond; ideas are not an end in themselves but are meant to render action possible in the domain of "the real." A fiction can thus be looked on as "a 'legitimatized error,' i.e. as a fictional conceptual construct that has justified its existence by its success."[5] It is, in fact, dangerous to invest a fiction with substantive truth. What happens often, especially in the realm of religion, is that what was originally intended as a bold figure of speech is converted in the course of time into a dogma. "The expression, 'I believe in God,' means simply that 'I act *as if* a God really existed.' "[6]

Though Vaihinger's theory of as-if fictions did not directly influence literature in the modern age, it helped to generate a climate of thought which, in collaboration with the philosophical contribution of Schopenhauer and Nietzsche, produced a shattering impact on the creative imagination. As I have already observed, Nietzsche struggled all his life with the problem of "truth" and formulated an aesthetic that recognized the fundamental importance of the will to illusion. Jules de Gaultier went beyond Nietzsche in exalting the will to illusion rather than the will to power. Like Vaihinger, Gaultier strips away all the phantom abstractions which thinkers hypostatize as if they were solid, self-sufficient realities. Like Nietzsche and Vaihinger, he questions the value of "truth." The craving for truth must give way before the craving for illusion, which is based on the need to celebrate life.

Relativism comes to a head in Gaultier's perception that life is an illusion viewed through the perspective of a particular sensibility. If life is illusion, the enemy of illusion is knowledge. The struggle between the two adversaries goes on. But illusion is never overthrown, for it serves to enhance life while knowledge is inimical to life. In the conflict between instinct and intellect, it is always instinct that triumphs in the end. History is but the record of the successive victories won by a variety of fictions or myths. Like Vaihinger, Gaultier contends that "thought creates Being. The concept of God creates God."[7] The categories of time, of space, and of causality are but part of the ongoing process of illusion.

This philosophy of relativism left its imprint in different ways on the literary imagination of our time. Writers like Gide and Montherlant, D. H. Lawrence and Aldous Huxley, Hemingway and Malraux, Sartre and Genet, Eugene O'Neill and Samuel Beckett, cannot reconcile the contradictions of existence; they find it impossible to solve the epistemological puzzle. Life in all its complex manifestations, the uprush of chthonic instincts, the eruption of Dionysian energy (and Euripides portrayed it long ago in his tragedy, the *Bacchae*), all this works havoc with the efforts man makes to determine his place in the universe. As Max Scheler says: "In the thousand years of history, we are the first age in which man has become utterly and unconditionally 'problematic' to himself, in which he no longer knows who he is, but at the same time *knows* that he does not know."[8] It is this realization, that man ceases to know himself and *knows* that he does not know, which precipitated a crisis of consciousness in the literature of our age. Everything was relativized: time and space, history and religion, morality and myth, and the mind which created them all.

In this cultural crisis Husserl's phenomenology appealed strongly to a number of writers, because it turned their attention away from the desert of abstract thought to the things themselves. Consciousness is directed toward a world which it can never possess. The world is there, before analysis supervenes. Man creates his own meaning and in doing so shapes his own history. "Because we are in the world, we are *condemned to meaning*."[9] If man is a unique being, he can only report what is true of his experience in time and place; he cannot presume to know and communicate the *whole* of existence. Consequently relativity of perception, like relativity of values, is not to be avoided. It is relativity that distinguishes the literature of Sartrean existentialism from preceding literary movements. The universe is seen not from some vantage point of the absolute but from our own situation in the world, from our position in space as well as in time. The phenomenological approach made possible not only the return to things but also the emergence of the idea of human freedom.

Combine this idea of the relativity of value with that of human freedom, and there is no longer any reason why man should not create his own values, why God should not be replaced by man. We are here at the very heart of our modern dilemma. Can a civilisation survive the extinction of its beliefs; must man believe in something beyond himself, or will he prove capable of creating and respecting his own laws?[10]

Some artists, notably the futurists, tried to force their way out of this spiritual impasse by worshiping a mystique of speed, motion, machinery, dynamism. This was the desperate strategy they resorted to in striving to bridge the gulf between the object and the mind, world and consciousness. Their obsession with speed and the dynamic principle was coupled, strangely enough, with a search for the universal and the abstract. Their awareness of motion, as it struggled to communicate the splendors and terrors of the visible universe, was extended to the cosmos as a whole. The "Initial Manifesto of Futurism," issued on February 20, 1909, declared its task to be the breaking down of the portals of the impossible. "Time and Space died yesterday. Already we live in the absolute, since we have already created speed, eternal and ever-present."[11]

Futurism, though it flourished for a brief period under the leadership of Marinetti, was an eccentric and abortive movement, but it illustrated the degree to which the theory of relativity had established itself in art as well as in literature. Writers seized on this revolution in science to support their intuitive belief that literature can never hope to capture life in its totality; only a selected portion can be given the shaped unity of an art form, and that form at best constitutes only a symbolic version. The Newtonian universe gives way steadily to a conception of the world of relativity as portrayed by nuclear physics. In his poems on Einstein and in other poems, MacLeish conveys a sense of infinite space, of a reality that has forever lost its material solidity. There are no longer any fixed points of reference. Absolute space, like absolute time, has disappeared. Einstein had dissolved the sensuous world of the poets "into a set of mathematical equations."[12]

Lost in empty space, knowing that there are no answers to the questions he must nevertheless ask, the writer essays to reveal some underlying pattern in the chaotic streaming of events. His work must at least *seem* real. He copes with this relativity of vision by presenting characters each of whom inhabits a private world of his own, so that the universe of experience he projects is "real" as seen from a particular perspective, and yet infinitely diverse. There is no universal human truth. If the modern novelist tries to follow the example of Flaubert and "be in his work like God in creation, invisible and omnipotent,"[13] he must refrain from pulling the strings that control the action of his characters, for by doing so he denies them their heritage of freedom. If he is to do full justice to the refractory body of his material, he must give up the luxury of being a privileged observer. Despite all his efforts to remain invisible, however, he cannot get rid of himself. The author, too, represents a point of view as he struggles to set forth the polarities of the relativistic vision.[14]

3. POINT COUNTER POINT

In searching for a fairly representative specimen of relativism in modern literature, one is faced with an embarrassment of riches. Among the secular writers of the twentieth century, how many could be called believers in the Absolute? Though they may not have studied the general or special theory of relativity, they assume that the physical world consists "of a four-dimensional manifold of events."[15] This is taken for granted and inevitably leaves its mark on their interpretation of experience. This is what Paul Elmer More fiercely attacks as the Demon of the Absolute, the deadly spirit of empirical rationalism inherited from the time of the Renaissance that pictures the world as composed of energy and thus deprives man of his supranatural status.[16] In particular, he is horrified by the attempt to represent life as an unmitigated flux, "which in practice, however it be in literature, means confinement in a mad-house."[17] Neither More's bitter protest nor that of Irving Babbitt and Wyndham Lewis could stem the flood. The perspective of relativism has triumphed in literature, so much so that there are few works of the imagination today that have not, in one way or another, been affected by it. Even modern poetry, according to Durrell, "unconsciously reproduces something like the space-time continuum in the way that it uses words and phrases: and the way in which its forms are cyclic rather than extended."[18]

The discoveries of science were bound to have a disintegrating effect on literature and art even before the ideas of Einstein had been assimilated by the popular mind. Cubism, surrealism, the stream-of-consciousness technique, expressionism, the elimination of auctorial commentary from the fictional narrative so that the novel becomes "pure" and autonomous: all these in a sense represented a reaction to relativism. In cubism, the painter went far out in the "dehumanization" of art, reducing the world to a series of mechanistic aspects. The human element dwindles steadily to a minimum;

for man is unnecessary as an object in the dissection of spatial relationships, vortices of converging planes, and all the complicated systems of abstraction that can be deduced. In total abstraction and in action-painting man is finally annihilated, liquidated. Self-alienation can go no further, except to the blank canvas, silence, death.[19]

The Cubist painter is interested not in the recognizable object in its phenomenological particularity but in releasing the unique way in which his creative vision functions, since he knows that what he looks upon is only a perspective. It is he who is responsible for investing matter with form. Like the physicists, he comes to realize that man, by virtue of observing nature, inevitably distorts it. The conception of matter as energy in perpetual flux results in a process of abstraction that practically excludes man from the universe.[20] The old tradition is abandoned. The hero is dead.

During the hectic twenties the dominant literary ideology was that of relativism. Relativism of knowledge entails a relativism of values. Only God is free of all illusion, except for the logical necessity of preserving the belief that he is God. Jung, in *Psychological Types*, discusses the relativity of the symbol in connection with the relativity of God to man.[21] Aldous Huxley, in *Do What You Will*, espouses a doctrine of relativism, one that welcomes inconsistencies and contradictions. He calls rationalism a vital lie. "A rational absolute is a contradiction in terms. The only absolute which a man of intelligence can believe in is an irrational one."[22] The life-worshiper—and Huxley professed to be that at this stage of his literary development—is at home with all his polarities of being; he is both positivist and mystic, pessimist and optimist, holding these different beliefs "because he is many different people."[23] One world view is as good and as true as another. Fundamentally, Huxley, like many of his contemporaries at the time, took it for granted

that there was no meaning. This was partly due to the fact that I shared the common belief that the scientific picture of an abstraction from reality was a true picture of reality as a whole; partly also to other, non-intellectual reasons. I had motives for not wanting the world to have a meaning; consequently assumed that it had none, and was able without any difficulty to find satisfying reasons for this assumption.[24]

In *Point Counter Point*, Huxley transforms relativity of perception into a supporting narrative technique. As in *The Counterfeiters* to which it bears a strong resemblance, the novel introduces a novelist who speculates on the structural possibilities open to the art of fiction. It is Philip Quarles who seeks to devise a new way of looking at things. For him this new approach is summed up by multiplicity: "multiplicity of eyes and multiplicity of aspects seen."[25] It is possible to interpret events as viewed from a clashing variety of perspectives: by a bishop, a merchant, a hedonist, a physicist, a Communist, a Fascist, a historian, a biologist. "Each sees, professionally, a different aspect of the event, a different layer of reality. What I want to do is to look with all those eyes at once. With religious eyes, scientific eyes, economic eyes, *homme moyen sensuel* eyes."[26] The symbolic portrayal of reality from these radically different and incommensurable perspectives is never so queer as the original reality, since "everything's implicit in anything,"[27] even the most commonplace object. Possessing what Keats calls "negative capability," Philip, like Huxley, could identify himself with the most assorted types of men, become mystic, humanitarian, saint, misanthrope. He could not, however, remain someone else; he often rebelled against this state of Pyrrhonian suspension. But he could not enjoy the privilege of being truly himself, for he did not know who he was.

Point Counter Point, the technique of whch owes much to *Ulysses* as well as *The Counterfeiters*, represents Huxley's effort to deal imaginatively with the destructive forces his age had unleashed. He develops his theme by exploiting the device of the musicalization of fiction, relying on strategic shifts in mood and point of view, counterpointing plot structure and characters, presenting simultaneity of contrasting effects and events of time, all designed to illustrate the relativistic motif that people react in different ways to the same problem. By placing a novelist within his novel, Huxley is able to include discursive pages of speculation on the aesthetics of fiction and the difficult task of portraying the nature of reality. What he seeks to achieve is a symphonic structure that will present varied types of character, each one justified in his own right. He combines "scientific" objectivity with a multiplicity of perspectives.

The character on whom Huxley lavishes the most loving strokes is Philip Quarles, who is in many respects a portrait of Huxley: the self-conscious skeptic, the aloof and secretive personality, the intellectual who is at home only in the world of ideas, emotionally unable to establish living contact with others. His notebooks, like Edouard's journal in *The Counterfeiters*, record his broodings, his introspections, his awareness of the universal flux and fusion. He wants to go beyond the realistic coordination of details. If he writes about the kitchen, he wants the description to vibrate with cosmic overtones; each sentence should suggest the history of the universe. Like Blake, he is aware, but only intellectually, of the whole creation present in a grain of sand. The whole story of the universe, he realizes, "is implicit in any part of it. The meditative eye can look through any simple object and see, as through a window, the entire cosmos."[28] From the smell of roast duck it is possible to travel to the spiral nebulae, to music, to martyrdom. Everything becomes odd, surrealistic, and incredible if the encrusted film of familiarity is removed. Every event "contains within itself an infinity of depths within depths. Nothing's in the least like what it seems—or rather it's like several million other things."[29] These observations, repeated like a leitmotif, offer a clue to the aesthetic of perspectivism Huxley held at the time.

Philip Quarles sets down his thoughts on the musicalization of fiction, finding hints for this in the work of a composer like Beethoven:

A novelist modulates by reduplicating situations and characters. He shows several people falling in love, or dying, or praying in different ways— dissimilars solving the same problem. Or, *vice versa*, similar people confronted with dissimilar problems. In this way you can modulate through all the aspects of your theme, you can write variations in any number of different moods. Another way: The novelist can assume the god-like creative privilege and simply elect to consider the events of the story in their various aspects—emotional, scientific, economic, religious, metaphysical, etc. He will modulate from one to the other—as, from the aesthetic to the physico-chemical aspect of things, from the religious to the physiological or financial.[30]

This is the method Huxley uses in endeavoring to apply the philosophy of relativism to the universe of fiction. The result of all of

Philip's introspections and philosophical gyrations is that he comes at the end to the discovery of the obvious: namely, that the intellectual life only substitutes formulas and abstractions for the disorderly complexities of living. Even the quest for truth can become an evasion of responsibility, a flight from life and love. What Philip, like his begetter, signally lacked was the wisdom of the heart. As Mark Rampion, the fictionalized version of D. H. Lawrence, cries out: the truth, the human truth, is discovered not by thought but by living. Philip's relativistic attitude toward life and people takes the form of a skepticism tempered by indifference.

Almost half a century has passed since D. H. Lawrence, in *Fantasia of the Unconscious* (1921), published before *Point Counter Point* appeared, took up the challenge posed by the latest scientific discovery, the theory of relativity. How to account for this curious craze? Lawrence endeavors to explain what it can mean for the popular mind. "There is no one single absolute central principle governing the world. The great cosmic forces or mechanical principles can only be known in their relation to one another, and can only exist in their relation to one another."[31] Lawrence, unlike Huxley, does not stand in awe before the authority of science; he reacts by vigorously voicing the hope that the theory will prove to be wrong. But the idea of relativity caught on rapidly; the universe has, consequently, begun to fall apart, since "there is nothing absolute left in the universe. Nothing."[32] Everything in the world of the twentieth century has become relativized. Instead of singling out the relativity theory for purposes of attack, most modern writers seem to take it more or less for granted. *The Chinese Wall* (1946), a play by Max Frisch that I shall discuss later, recognizes that the most revolutionary advance in the world has been made in the field of science, namely, the discovery that "energy equals mass times the speed of light squared. Whereby the speed of light (one hundred eighty-six thousand miles a second) is the single absolute power with which we are able to reckon nowadays. Everything else, we know, is relative."[33] *The Chinese Wall* reflects the crisis of consciousness—and conscience—brought about by the dropping of the atomic bombs on Hiroshima and Nagasaki.

As this crisis of consciousness grew more widespread and more acute, many contemporary writers were led to view the world through a perspective that is often comic and ironic; they suffered profoundly from the lack of an overall, integrating vision. Relativism has become so "deeply ingrained in twentieth-century culture that it permeates even the popular novel sold at the railway bookstall or the airline terminal."[34] The baffling problem with which the modern writer is burdened is how to voice some saving imaginative truth even though he knows, like Capek, that he cannot find truth. The literary relativist cuts the Gordian knot not by trying to view the universe of experience through the perspective of reason but by frankly embracing art as illusion. Life is a dream, a gamble, a game, a theater of magic and make-believe, a form of madness, the product of a diseased consciousness.

Is all that we see or seem
But a dream within a dream?

—EDGAR ALLAN POE
"A Dream within a Dream"

1. THE MYSTERIOUSNESS OF REALITY

OF THE INFINITELY VARIED masks that life may wear, one of the most ancient and most beguiling is that of the dreamer caught within the confines of a dream. The imagination then comes into its own as the eye of creative vision. External reality is abolished. The voice of solipsism seems to offer the only truth worthy of credence, but even that is to be doubted since the dreamer knows or suspects he is only dreaming. Strindberg, in his expressionistic plays, heightened the force of subjectivity to a degree where the world becomes hallucinatory and apparitional. In *A Dream Play*, matter dissolves, disintegrated by the X-ray of spirit; time and space are confounded; past and present mysteriously fuse in the alembic of memory. The only thing that reconciles all contradictions in the strange world of the dream is the ego of the dreamer. Breaking away from the Procrustean criteria of realism, expressionism projects characters who are types, or numbers, or symbols, or even abstract pronouns. Reacting against the stereotyped conception of reality as it is portrayed by naturalism, it exploits the power of the irrational and introduces heroes whose quest for the

29

absolute is brought to a halt in the quicksands of subjectivity.[1]

If the writer relies principally on the dream metaphor to convey his awareness of a reality that is beyond cognition, he is plagued, like the expressionists, by the difficulty of communicating his vision of the infinite in aesthetically satisfying terms. The symbol is the richly ambiguous means by which the ineffable can find its objective correlative. It provides numberless ways of interpreting the fate of the human dreamer and of the dream that is life. Here is a perspective which, though originally owing nothing to the influence of science, can, as in surrealist poetry and art, make good "unconscious" use of the discoveries of psychoanalysis and shadow forth a world that is marvelous, irrational, and beautifully absurd. The hero as dreamer may be engaged in the search for God or the absolute or for the ultimate mystery, as in *The Wanderer* by Alain-Fournier, that represents the lost paradise of childhood.[2]

Fournier, the artist as dreamer, hated intellectual abstractions and dwelt by preference in the world of the imagination. His method of writing fiction was similar to that employed by Maeterlinck in his early plays, but with the difference that Fournier concentrated, as did Kafka, on realistic details; the structure of his tale, however, is shot through with the vital element of fantasy. He beheld life as a moving dream, and it was the dream that informed his masterpiece and constituted the reality of the past and his anticipation of the future.[3] Bathed in an aura of magic, the novel departs, like Proust's work, from the method of realism. Though it works out the medieval theme of the quest, the logic of the dream governs much of the plot of *The Wanderer* as it endeavors to capture intimations of the infinite in the net of language. Fournier equates the dream with memory, utilizing the indefinite as a means of symbolically revealing some haunting aspects of the mystery of being.[4]

Or the hero as dreamer may be a creature of instinct, driven by the libido, galvanized into action by impulses that have their origin in the depths of the unconscious. Or he may be delineated as a puppet pulled by invisible strings from behind the stage, so that his strutting and striving, his ranting and twitching, act out an idiotic comedy. Man is an embodied fiction in the drama of a dream, but it is hard to make out who composes the script, how the various roles are assigned. Is the dialogue largely improvised as in a *commedia dell'arte*, or rehearsed beforehand, or whispered by the omniscient prompter? Life is then essentially a marionette show, though to the individual involved in the plot it may appear as a tragedy.

The external world in which man finds himself poses an epistemological enigma. What is nature, and to what extent is it transformed by the perceptions of the beholder? The older confident relationship between man and the universe has been destroyed. Modern man feels lost in the infinite spaces; the multiplicity of phenomena fills him with a sense of cosmic alienation. He cannot determine which metaphysical perspective is the right one, that is, closer to "the truth" of reality. It is this very assumption of "objective" truth that perspectivism rejects; there is no single, definitive version of reality. Every perception, in the dream or waking state, is refracted through the prism of a given temperament. There is only a human reality, and that differs from one individual to another; each person, as Proust reveals in *Remembrance of Things Past*, is a private universe. Hence life does not yield one and only one meaning. It means different things to different people, and it may mean different things to the same person at different stages of his development.

2. PROUST AND MEMORY

The magical evocation of memory provided Proust with the method he was seeking and confirmed his intuitive knowledge of the relativity of the self. His imagination was so constituted that it could interpret relativity "truly" only in the enchanting vista of time past. He described these epiphanies of memory again and again, fascinated by the transmutation of reality they effect. They are mystical states which afford him an awareness of the timeless essence of things. Proust thus works out in his fiction a challenging philosophy of reality, which is beheld through the spectrum of subjectivity.

He was not interested in realism or naturalism, in propaganda, social causes, the stormy issues of politics. Like Maeterlinck, he believed that true art is born in silence. Subjective impressions are creatively more nourishing than ideologies. The only reality that exists for each of us is our own sensitivity to impressions, and these are to be found not in the world of space but in the self. Fiction that plumes itself on its rigorous fidelity to objective data is the farthest removed from reality, according to Proust. Since the essence of being is in large part subjective, it cannot be communicated. Literary realism fails in its aim because reality cannot be defined as a photographic copy. Realism, in fact, perpetuates a lie. The grandeur of art lies preeminently in its ability to put us in touch with a reality that is hidden but ultimate. Proust persuasively sets forth the theme of perspectivism to which this book is addressed:

Only by art can we get outside ourselves, know what another sees of his universe, which is not the same as ours and the different views of which would otherwise have remained as unknown to us as those there may be on the moon. Thanks to art, instead of seeing only one world, our own, we see it under multiple forms, and as many as there are original artists, just so many worlds have we at our disposal.[5]

But this world of the imagination that art delineates is not to be confused with the world which we automatically inhabit. Art, by breaking the grip of habit, allows us to penetrate to those arcane depths where reality lies hidden. To capture this secret life of the spirit the writer must abandon his belief in the objectivity of the world. If dreams had always fascinated Proust, that is because they made so vivid the subjective nature of his most poignant experiences and overthrew the tyranny of mechanical time.

Sleep for Proust produces a more profound and authentic revelation of reality than does consciousness. Life changes from year to year, day to day; we are never the same. Imagination makes fools of us all. The persons we once loved are not now as they were when we knew them in the past—a form of psychological relativism that Durrell develops in the *Alexandria Quartet.* Only in sleep is the iron law that governs public time annulled. Proust is haunted by "the internal dialogue of memories and the incessant verbiage of sleep."[6] The hero of *Cities of the Plain* realizes that it is his fate "to pursue only phantoms, creatures whose reality existed to a great extent in my imagination."[7]

In Proust's novels, the inward life, like the unconscious, creates its own oppressive phantoms. He found the most fruitful source of inventiveness in the world of dreams. "The universe," he declares, "is true for us all and dissimilar to each of us."[8] "The only true voyage of discovery . . . would be not to visit strange lands but to possess other eyes, to behold the universe through the eyes of another, of a hundred others, to behold the hundred universes that each of them beholds, that each of them is."[9] Here, eloquently summed up, is the dizzy, dazzling vision of a galaxy of universes, each one autonomous and unique. The world is as the subjective eye apprehends it. Our memories, desires, and dreams permeate and color all our perceptions. Though the experiment of Proust in fiction probably owed nothing to Einstein's theory of relativity, his "treatment of memory, as always multiple, implies a relativity principle in consciousness."[10]

3. MAETERLINCK AND THE THEATER OF SILENCE

The mystical vision is born of the realization that there are more things between heaven and earth than are apparent to the eye of reason. A leaf of grass, Whitman believes, is no less than the journey work of the stars, and a mouse "is miracle enough to stagger sextillions of infidels." To the mind of the visionary poet the phenomenon of life is a perpetual source of wonder. It simply *is*; it cannot be explained in terms of "why." But man is nevertheless eager to spell out, if he can, the meaning of the strange world he lives in. Facts and empirical data alone cannot satisfy his metaphysical hunger. Events take place in the world, but there is also a psychic universe which internalizes and interprets each event. Moments of luminous insight occur when the mind suddenly seems to see into the heart of things. But these epiphanies may be negative in character. Like Mrs. Moore's experience in the Marabar Caves in *A Passage to India*, when she was overcome by the echoing sound of "Boum," they may suggest the meaninglessness of all aspiration and endeavor. The symbolists strove to discern the dim outlines of the beyond, the presence of the eternal in the fleeting instant. Like Maeterlinck, however, they could not transcend the aesthetic stage. As Kierkegaard could have taught them, it is not possible, through the mediation of art, to reach the absolute. Maeterlinck beheld the mystery that words cannot translate, the strangeness of reality that science cannot account for, but he could not get himself to believe that the life of man was anything more than a dream.

The romantic poets had been captivated by the music of silence, the beauty of the ineffable, which language cannot hope to communicate. To the clairvoyant gaze of a Baudelaire, appearances disclose the haunting symbols of a suprasensible world. Mallarmé, too, disintegrated the established concept of reality and sought contact with the realm of the unknown. Maeterlinck wished to suggest the mystical overtones of silence, but silence, unfortunately, does not exist as a separate, communicable language. It can be communicated, if at all, only through the refractory medium of words resonant with intimations of the silence that surrounds all efforts at speech. The drama of silence does not, of course, exist. Silence is not poetry or drama. However much Maeterlinck experiments with the evocative power of the mystique of silence, he is still compelled to make use of language, though like Alain-Fournier he uses language in order to call forth an image of reality as the realm of the mysterious.

Maeterlinck was at the beginning of his career temperamentally drawn to symbolism. Through the influence of Villier de l'Isle Adam and his tragedy, *Axel*, Maeterlinck was led to explore the mystical side of life, even though he had left Christianity and its hope of redemption forever behind him. In 1889, he composed *The Intruder*, in which death is the expected visitor, waited for with terrible foreboding. Time spells out the span of life, a minuscule fraction of the eternal. In *The Blind*, completed in 1890, death is once more the "hero." An old priest dies and leaves the band of blind people leaderless. They are terrified, but then a mysterious stranger—death himself—arrives on the scene and releases them from the clutch of terror. Though he had lost his religious faith, Maeterlinck, the mystic, cannot withdraw from the contemplation of the invisible world, the occult forces—he calls them destiny—that govern the lives of men. Destiny is inscrutable and hostile; man is helpless in his struggle against it. Here is a vision of man as a fated victim, bewildered, defenseless, and alone. The "static theater" Maeterlinck labored to create depicts the tragedy of the bereft and helpless soul.

Maeterlinck tries to make drama do the impossible: to convey through the language of symbols and gestures, mood and atmosphere, the abiding mystery of life and death. He deploys words as well as portents, sounds in the night, passing shadows, to suggest the nature of the invisible. A pause, a moment of waiting, an attitude of strained listening for a sound or a step, the guttering of a lamp, the fall of darkness, the faint flutter of wings, the dropping of a leaf to the ground, all this is intended to reveal a reality that is not only beyond rational comprehension but instinct with terror. In *The Intruder* it is the blind grandfather who is aware of the invisible forces that the others, more naïvely trusting in their perceptions of the world, fail to see. And when the aged grandfather falls asleep, it is the uncle, strangely enough, who sounds this Maeterlinckian motif: "Not to know where one is, not to know whence one has come, not to know whither one is going, no longer to distinguish midday from midnight, nor summer from winter . . . . And always that darkness, that darkness! . . . I would rather not live."[11]

Nothing really happens in the play. The clock continues to strike the hour. (In Ionesco's theater of the absurd, the clock strikes erratically so that even the dimension of time is unpredictable.) The grandfather is convinced that the truth is being kept from him. "I am here, all alone," he cries out, "in darkness without end!"[12] It is the cry of deluded mankind. When he demands to know the truth, the uncle replies: "But there is no truth!"[13] The grandfather hears noises; the lamplight flickers unsteadily, the room is plunged in darkness, and in the darkness the effect of silence is intensified. The hour of midnight strikes and death finally makes his entry.

The Blind also sets forth the hopeless condition of mankind. The priest, who took the group of the blind on a journey through the woods, is dead, and they, in their blindness, cannot find the way back. They sit waiting, surrounded by funereal trees bathed in moonlight. They are aware of each other only by the sound of their voices. Though the priest (they do not know that he is sitting among them, dead) has told them to wait for him in silence, they must speak. The Second Blind Man (the characters are not individualized) says, "We ought to know where we are!"[14] The Very Old Man replies: "We cannot know!"[15] Though they try to reassure themselves that all is well, they are frightened, like the rest of mankind, by their apprehension of the unknowable.

Then, in the far distance, a clock strikes twelve strokes slowly (Maeterlinck repeatedly uses the symbol of the clock as a *memento mori*), but the blind are not sure whether it is noon or midnight. The Very Old Man declares: "We have never seen each other. We ask and we reply; we live together, we are always together, but we know not what we are!"[16] That is their tragedy, not knowing what they are, and it anticipates the absurd plight of the antihero of our day. The Very Old Man repeats his dolorous complaint: "You would say we were forever alone!"[17] Like the grandfather in *The Intruder*, it is the Very Old Blind Man who senses that someone is there. At the end they hear footsteps; their deliverer approaches, but he responds to neither question nor pleas for pity. And then silence falls.

The knowledge of the inevitability of death, which obsessed Maeterlinck throughout his life, conditioned his view of reality. This was the dark mystery he sought in vain to penetrate. Like other explorers of what lies beyond the reach of consciousness, he was defeated in his quest. All one could know was what one experienced between birth and death, and then the curtain rang down, the play was over. There was no guarantee that the dream play would run its course to the last act. Death threatens us at every moment; it is the supreme fact that surrounds life. As Maeterlinck declares in *Our Eternity*: "The more we dread it, the more dreadful it becomes, for it but thrives on our fears."[18] Despite all human endeavors to pluck out the heart of the mystery, death remains unknown and therefore life remains unknown.

But the mind, though hurled back from its assaults on the frontiers of the unknown, returns again and again to the attack. It cannot rest in mystery; it seeks to break out of the dream. It cannot but find death hateful. It is hateful because it brings life to an abrupt, ignominious end. Death is linked with nameless terror because it plunges man into the gulf of the unknown. How can death result in total annihilation? "We can no more conceive death than we can conceive nothingness."[19] As for the survival of personal consciousness—that is a dreamed-of wish without reality. Maeterlinck beholds a universe that is without beginning and without end and without purpose. The force that rules the universe (it is not directed by intelligence) cannot be grasped by thought. The secret of the universe is not to be discovered.

Maeterlinck touches the depths of despair as he dwells on the finality of death. He studied theosophy, Hinduism, spiritualism, the occult, but saw no reason for believing in the truth of any of them. Though he cherished no hope of survival after death, he came in time to rely more and more on intuition. He adhered, however, to no system of thought. In his old age he became convinced that ignorance is man's fate. Despite all the researches of science, the universe remains unfathomable. Peering into the depths of the unknown in the hope of deciphering its secret, all he discovers is that man is not in control of his destiny. As a recent critic of his work remarks:

He failed to penetrate the mysteries of Destiny and Death, he did not discover the universal secret of wisdom and truth, nor capture the blue bird of happiness. In all the ways he trod he found no joy, but only greater ignorance. And in the end he could only make confession of his own failure.[20]

As a dramatist who experimented with the symbolism of silence and the dream perspective, Maeterlinck is more important for what he attempted than for what he achieved. He tried not only to probe the interior life of people, their nostalgias, their spiritual phobias and obsessions, but also to create a dream-world in which reality and unreality merge. It is not so much what his characters say that is arresting as what they are in various ways striving to suggest: the mystery and the tragedy of life. That is why Maeterlinck concentrates attention on the essence rather than the accidents of human nature. He gives up all interest in the problem of causation in order to hold up an image of the surrealist strangeness of the familiar. Drama, fused with poetry, is meant to communicate that which is left unspoken and which cannot perhaps be uttered: the esoteric language of the soul, its quest, however deluded, for the absolute.

The patent weaknesses of symbolic drama of this kind are, as in expressionism, connected with its approach to reality. It is difficult for language to express the lineaments of the invisible world. As Andreyev points out in his analysis of Maeterlinck's work, the symbolic form lends itself admirably to the presentation of ideas, but it falls lamentably short in the field of psychological motivation. The symbolist does not present, he states. His plays must be taken on faith or else they fail completely to induce a willing suspension of disbelief. As Andreyev says: "Maeterlinck does not prove, he only commands."[21]

But there is actually no need for proof. To behold the spectacle of life as the unfolding drama of a dream is in itself an example of perspectivism in action. The dream reveals that what man takes for granted as the solid structure of reality is only an illusion. It is the dream that holds up an image of what is ultimately real. The dream, a dissolvent of certitudes, breaks up the regularity of chronological time. Then, too, the dream perspective transcends the fixed limits set by reason. As the dreamer is, so is the character of his dream of life. If for Unamuno the life of man is but a dream of God, for Maeterlinck the life of man is a frightening dream that ends in silence. Both writers assume that the dream is the true reality, but Unamuno's dream creates God whereas Maeterlinck's dream, for all its obscurantist mysticism, rejects the possibility of faith. The dreamer, in any case, seizes upon those views which are congenial to his own spirit. In Proust the dreamer gives birth to himself. The dream perspective brings to light a vision of reality that prepares us for the revelations of the unconscious.

1. *THE POINT OF VIEW OF SURREALISM*

THE BELIEF that life is a dream affords no indication of what implications the writer will draw from it. Freud's *Interpretation of
Dreams* opened the gates of understanding to a fantastic dream-
world. His theory of repression, his exploration of the unconscious
and the underground of the neuroses, enabled a host of poets, dramatists, and novelists to view reality through the distorting lens
of the irrational and the abnormal. A strange paradox was involved
in this literary development. Psychoanalysis, priding itself on being
a science, adhered to a positivistic conception of reality. Its therapeutic method labored to adjust man to a dynamic, deterministic
universe that is forever subject to change. Those who grasp the
scientific vision of the world give up the notion of free will and
come to realize that they are part of a natural cycle of causation.[1]
Psychoanalysis assumed that "reality" is open to empirical inquiry,
that reality, as opposed to illusion, is scientific reality, and that art
represents a form of dreaming and wish-fulfillment.

The surrealist point of view, its aesthetic based on the psychoanalytic discovery of the unconscious and the creative energies

presumably stored there, went far beyond its Freudian antecedents. It drew inspiration from the Dionysian philosophy of Nietzsche, the mystical vision of Blake, the biological pessimism of Schopenhauer, the poetry of Lautréamont and Rimbaud, and the metaphysics of Bergson. What the surrealists did was to accord instinct primacy over consciousness, to make imagination prevail over reason. In poetry and art, they attempted to give expression to the night side of life. For the logic of science they substituted "the metalogic" of the unconscious.[2]

The surrealists were only partly indebted to psychoanalysis. They reacted against science by deliberately cultivating the soil of the irrational. Like Dostoevski's underground man, they rebelled against a Newtonian and Euclidian universe. They struggled to create a new interpretation of reality beheld from a multiplicity of "original" points of view, especially as glimpsed through the magical eye of the unconscious. Rejecting the categories of reason, they sought to pierce the mystery of the universe and engage in the quest for superreality, absolute reality. They invoked the thaumaturgy of dreams as a means of defeating the principle of causality. That is how they overthrew the philosophy of determinism, on which Freudianism was based, and enlisted the dream in the service of literature and art. In its efforts to transcend the limits of reason and "objective" reality, surrealism searched deliriously for new sources of beauty, the most strangely dissimilar objects being yoked together in a surprising image, like the one by Lautréamont: "Beautiful like the fortuitous meeting, on a dissection table, of a sewing machine and an umbrella."[3]

After passing through an early experimental stage of exploiting the resources of the unconscious, the surrealists made the attempt to fuse interior and external reality. In 1925 they suddenly decided on the necessity of bridging the gap between absolute idealism and dialectical materialism. This marriage of opposites could not be consummated. Though André Breton, the leader of the movement, refused to surrender to the demand that poetry and art become the vehicles of propaganda, the merger with Marxism weakened the cause of surrealism and proved ill-fated. The surrealists could not retain their old unalloyed faith in the power of inspiration and the irrational and at the same time hope to satisfy the dogmatic requirements of communist ideology. Louis Aragon, a former surrealist converted to communism, denounced the surrealists severely for failing to become dialectical materialists:

I proclaim the return to reality. Enough of games, enough of day dreams, to the kennels with your phantasies, diurnal and nocturnal! Do you not see whither you are being led by this liberty of experience which you complacently claim? Are there not those among you who have ended by loving "experience" so much that they have seen even in the torture chambers of the Nazis, in the Hitler rods and axes, interesting accessories of vice, human values after all? You have not the courage to sweep all that away, to render it justice, because in your unfortunate heads you carry contradictions which are like contrary winds.[4]

Away, he earnestly urges them, from abominations like futurism, drugs to deaden the pain of ennui, desperate distractions, flights from the challenge of reality, all of which lead to fascism. "Bread and work!"—that is the salvationary slogan to which they must respond. The choice they must make is one between socialist realism and the untenable idealism of the surrealist aesthetic. Here we are able to behold two radically conflicting conceptions of reality as they engage in competition for the allegiance of the artist.

But the initial and enduring motive power of surrealism lay in its adherents' yearning to be reabsorbed in the life of nature. The surrealists experimented with psychic automatism in order to allow the unconscious to work in unfettered freedom of inspiration. In revolt against rational reality, they flatly denied that the creations of the mind corresponded with the structure of the world. The scientific principle of indeterminacy served to underline the limitations of the intellect. Things are not what they seem to common sense. Transfiguring every object of perception, dreams changed the familiar world of reality into a kingdom of the marvelous and the uncanny. In this irrational and indeterminate universe, "the most improbable happenings seem normal, the critical spirit is abolished, and constraints vanish. This enchanted world is truly that of Surreality."[5]

In its manifestos, its paintings and poetry, surrealism projected a reality that is not only protean, full of surprises, but unknowable. Since the categories of time and space, the conditions which make all knowledge possible, are but mind-born entities, the thing-in-itself cannot be grasped. The further back the surrealist artist pushed the frontiers of being, the more astonishing were the discoveries he made. The images rushing up from depths far below the level of consciousness disclose versions of reality beyond the scope of the five senses. It is the dream that furnishes an authentic, however fantastic, picture of the true reality. Dream and object, self and landscape blend; madness, like psychic automation, makes possible communion with the infinite. The object is "no longer to express or even to transform reality, but to surpass it and reach a world invisible to mortal eyes."[6]

2. ART AND DISEASE

If the psychoanalytic interpretation of art was correct, if the creative impulse was but a means of sublimating ungratified instincts, then the artist as confessed neurotic was bound in some measure to suffer an impairment of his will to create. There were, after all, other less painful and more rewarding methods of sublimation. At the worst, the "sick" artist could always turn to the psychoanalyst for therapeutic aid instead of forcing the unconscious to give birth to a grotesquely distorted, if not pathological, version of reality. In the tug-of-war between psychoanalysis and art, it was evident that the power of science, as the most reliable way of arriving at the reality-principle, would eventually tend to discredit art.

Sooner or later the artists were bound to revolt against the Freudian thesis that art was fundamentally a neurotic product. A number of writers rebelled against all the frightening talk of repressions that Freud brought to light: "Gagged, bound, maniacal repressions, sexual complexes, faecal inhibitions, dream-monsters."[7] D. H. Lawrence simply affirmed what he needed to believe, despite the restrictive norms of sanity the Freudians sought to impose. He did not care how these vital beliefs arose or if, when measured by the scientific reality-principle, they stood condemned as illusions. They were absolutely necessary for his life and art, and that was sufficient justification for cherishing them.

If Freud as a scientist endeavored to show how reality could be mastered, writers like Lawrence pressed home the question that is so crucial in our age of relativism: What is reality? Is the scientist so sure that he has unmasked the ultimate secret of life? What is normal and what is abnormal? Are they not, as Georg Groddeck maintained, strictly relative terms? Which is myth and which is reality? A mechanistic universe, determined in all its parts, is sterile and dreadfully boring. Lawrence found fault with Freudianism on the ground that it was too intellectualistic; he deeply distrusted the arbitrary constructions of the logical mind. The artist, who can get along very well without the midwifery of Freud, must follow his intuitions and depend on his own genius. Science is not salvation; knowledge is not life; art is not disease.[8]

The surrealists paid no heed to Lawrence's spirited protest. If the artist is neurotic by nature and neuroses make for heightened vision, then they were ready, like the shaman who is roused by drugs to a state of mystical frenzy, to capitalize on their neuroses. Abnormality is a virtue, madness a form of freedom. If they fail to abjure madness, it is because madness is uncontrollable, but they do not renounce their affiliation with psychopathology. *The Secret Life of Salvador Dali* brilliantly exemplifies the statement by Arthur Rimbaud that he ended by finding the disorder of his mind sacred. In this surrealist autobiography, the apotheosis of the abnormal, Dali "has transformed madness into a demoniacal creative principle."[9]

It is, of course, perfectly possible for an artist like Swift or Carroll or Kafka to be neurotic while his art, even when it views the world through the psychopathological perspective, represents a triumph of transcendence. The artist is productive in spite of, not because of, his neurotic constitution. As Jung remarks: "Disease has never yet fostered creative work; on the contrary, it is the most formidable obstacle to creation."[10] If some artists accept the conception of themselves as "neurotic," that is because their occupational role makes them feel guilty—a theme that crops up in the fiction of Kafka and in the early "decadent" stories of Thomas Mann. Though Freud had no intention of disparaging the constructive value of art, he did considerable damage by insisting that the artist was neurotic by nature.[11]

The exploitation of psychic disease for creative ends is by no means new. The relationship between the romantic temper and various psychopathological manifestations has been thoroughly examined by Mario Praz in *The Romantic Agony*. But at no time in the past did the exploitation of disease become the basis, scientifically supported, of an aggressive aesthetic and a comprehensive philosophy of life. That, however, is precisely what the surrealists attempted to do as they struggled to capture the elusive and equivocal truth of superreality. In the heady excitement of making new creative discoveries and experimenting with new forms of expression, they produced a literature infected with the will to disease.[12]

In their efforts to see into the heart of superreality, the literary surrealists tried to take down faithfully whatever the genius of the unconscious dictated. Like those members of the beat generation who resort to drugs in order to stimulate the free flow of the imagination, they induced hypnotic sleep and jotted down the oracular inspirations that streamed forth. Dreams, deliriously incoherent images, the elements of the absurd, the jetsam and flotsam thrown up by the tides of the unconscious, states of simulated madness— these were the magical ingredients that could give birth to a new art. Surrealism became in many instances, notably in the case of Salvador Dali, a militantly neurasthenic cult. Its flight from reason and the kind of impoverished reality that reason discloses turns out in practice to be little more than an obsession with the aberrations of the sexual instinct. Like the decadents in France, the surrealists exploited perversions in order to strengthen their debilitated sense of life.

3. THE SICKNESS OF ALIENATION

Whether or not disease provides a plenary source of mystical vision, there can be no doubt that the artist in our time feels cut off from his culture. By setting himself in opposition to it, he becomes more and more alienated from the world. He is not only a lonely prophet stoned by the populace for his heresies or his "abnormalities," he tends to use writing as a strategic substitute for living in "reality." Thomas Mann depicts artists who are "decadent" in their inability to root themselves in the life of their age. Adopting a spectatorial attitude, they utilize every personal experience as grist for the mill of their art. Influenced by Schopenhauer and that masterly psychologist of decadence, Nietzsche, Thomas Mann is identified with the portrait he draws of decadent artists: Tonio Kröger and Aschenbach, for example, who are but observers of existence. Even before writing *The Magic Mountain*, Thomas Mann had explored the relationship of genius to disease. The artist is inspired to create by virtue of his constructive abnormality. Disease and health, like life and death, are locked in battle.

Mann discerns a trace of the abnormal in that writers are generally isolated from the common life of mankind, that they love to dwell upon the symptoms of their suffering, brooding miserably and yet proudly on their fate of alienation. Branded with guilt because of his isolation, the artist is considered "queer," a freak of nature. Mann, however, did not surrender to the demons of the irrational; he was able to conquer the temptations that beset the romantic artist: his love of the night, his exaltation of feeling over reason, his attraction to the irrational aspects of experience. Though Mann curiously examined the potentialities of disease, his essay on Freud voices the hope that psychoanalysis will lead to the development of "a riper art than any possible in our neurotic, fear-ridden, hate-ridden world."[13]

Death in Venice, the story of an obsession, describes the awakening of homosexual love in a successful writer of fifty. Once Aschenbach lays eyes on a handsome Polish youth, he is lost; his madness is stronger than his reason. But his creative élan springs to life again. Mann calls attention to the often sickly condition of mind from which a "beautiful" work of art issues. "Who shall unriddle the puzzle of the artist nature? Who understands that mingling of discipline and licence in which it stands so deeply rooted?"[14] *Tonio Kröger* continues Mann's study of the alienated artist. Tonio, from the beginning, finds himself singled out because he is different from the others. The practice of art enables him to penetrate to the heart of things, shows him "the inwardness of the world and the ultimate behind men's words and deeds. And all that he saw could be put in two words: the comedy and the tragedy of life."[15]

Tonio, after leaving his native town, yields to the importunate demands of the flesh, though he struggles against the sensuality that has taken him captive. He swings between the two extremes of cold intellect and unbridled sensuality. But his suffering contributes to the making of his art; his creative powers grow more sensitively attuned. He gives himself completely to his work, "having no regard for himself as a human being but only as a creator."[16] Tonio, who expresses many of the ideas that Thomas Mann himself held on the subject of literature and reality, is aware that the so-called normal man is not interested in the arts. Tonio feels like an exile, excluded from participation in the life of mankind; he is sick to death "of depicting humanity without having any part or lot in it."[17] Set apart from others by virtue of his "priestly" calling, the writer ceases to be human.

Mann again makes the point that people who worship genius fail to realize that the unique gift which sustains the artist rests upon insecure, if not sinister, foundations. Mann describes sympathetically the struggle that takes place in the soul of Tonio who, despite everything, loves life, not the extraordinary but the normal, "life, in all its seductive banality!"[18] Far from being attracted by the perverse and the satanic, he longs "for a little friendship, devotion, familiar human happiness . . . for the bliss of the commonplace."[19] He is, as his friend points out, a bourgeois gone astray.

The artist, according to Thomas Mann, suffers because he cannot yield to this temptation "to live free from the curse of knowledge and the torment of creation, live and praise God in blessed mediocrity!"[20] Thomas Mann's exacting sense of duty, his own "bourgeois" conscience, led him to detect something unsavory, if not evil, in the life of art. Creativity is an affliction, a disease, a compulsion from which the writer would dearly like to escape. He suffered from the unnerving suspicion that writing is an illicit or neurotic deviation from the human norm. In an essay on Thomas Mann (1913), D. H. Lawrence, discussing *Tonio Kröger* and *Death in Venice*, condemns the latter as absolutely unwholesome, as offering a genuine portrait of "one sick vision."[21]

Nietzsche and Freud are unquestionably the most powerful influences on Thomas Mann in his treatment of the complex relation of art to disease in *The Magic Mountain*. Hans Castorp, the protagonist, is initiated into the mysteries of love, time, and death; the characters he meets in the Hans Berghof, the sanatorium for the tubercular, represent diseased Western civilization. Observing these patients, he arrives at the conclusion that there is no convincing evidence of the ennobling influence of disease, and yet disease, when it attacked his body, had awakened him spiritually. Disease had its fascinating, transcendental aspects. He decides to cast his lot with the world of the sick. But in the course of his stay on the heights, he comes to perceive that those who give in to the seduction of disease court destruction. At the end he reaches out decisively toward the goal of health. *The Magic Mountain* records Mann's inner struggle as an artist, his renunciation of the psychopathological perspective for creative ends; Hans Castorp is essentially the author himself.[22] In *The Magic Mountain* as in *Doctor Faustus*, Thomas Mann combated and overcame that which most strongly tempted him.

4. THE LURE OF MADNESS

I have examined some cases of the fascination of the perverse, the spell which the creative potentialities of disease exercised over surrealist writers and painters. If men like Dostoevski, Kierkegaard, Lautréamont, Nietzsche, and their twentieth-century descendants were interested in the phenomenology of madness it was because they saw in this state one way of escape from the dominant philosophy of "the normal" and "the real." The surrealists tried to break out of the intolerable world of the logical by instigating the imagination of the unconscious, thus producing an art that was antipositivistic, antinaturalistic, and antiscientific in its orientation. Like Dostoevski's underground man, they could not resign themselves to a principle of universal determinism or feel at home in a world that functioned with unfailing regularity like a machine. Abhorrent was the belief that the laws of mathematics are the laws of God.

If a number of modern artists embrace the irrational, it is because they are determined to throw off the scientific straitjacket of mechanical causation. If this be madness, then they will make the most of it. In order to release their powers of imagination in a spirit of freedom, they will go to any lengths to shatter the myth of "the objective." They refuse to believe that life is summed up by the biological or mechanical metaphor. In rebelling against the constricting doctrine of determinism, they are not only attempting to perceive reality in a new light, they are also engaged in shaping a new definition of man. Life is more than the colloidal organization of matter; it is magic and dream and mystery. Hence their efforts to rediscover the sources of spontaneity, to recapture the primitive purity of perception, to experiment with the creative potentialities of disease. Forms die as soon as they are born and hence should not be imitated; nothing repeats itself in the eternal flux. Modern writers are driven by the need to understand themselves and the world they live in, but they are convinced that such understanding is not to be gained by the exercise of reason. They must go beyond, always beyond, and somehow deal with a reality that is mystifying and absurd because it is, ultimately, incomprehensible.

The recent enthronement of the myth of the absurd is an acknowledgment of the insuperable limits of the intellect; it is a recognition of the unknowable, and therefore mysterious, nature of reality. The empty spaces that affrighted the mathematical-mystical mind of Pascal still have the power to affright modern man. The intervening centuries have not dissipated the terror of death or the *horror vacui*. Whereas myth and religion in the past brought man into vital symbolic relation to the cosmos and thus stripped it of much of its terror, these have today lost their efficacy. Lawrence's *Apocalypse* is a poignant lament for the death of this mythic consciousness and at the same time a desperate effort to bring it back to life.

The prophetic writers of the preceding century had struggled to reinstate these redemptive myths. The underground man of Dostoevski violently defied the categories of rationalism. This anti-hero flies in the face of logic; he contemptuously rejects the norms of sanity and the truths of mathematics. Vehemently he denies that two times two makes four. If one were to make two times two equal five, then this would be a mighty fine thing. The underground man is the discoverer of the chaos of the absurd. With perverse but nonetheless compelling passion he challenges the ruling materialistic ideology of his age:

> And why are you so firmly, so triumphantly convinced that only the normal and the positive—in other words, only what is conducive to welfare—is for the advantage of man? Is not reason in error as regards advantage? Does not man, perhaps, love something besides well-being? Perhaps he is just as fond of suffering? Perhaps suffering is just as great a benefit to him as well-being? Man is sometimes extraordinarily, passionately in love with suffering . . . . I hold no brief for suffering nor for well-being either. I am standing for . . . my caprice.[23]

Dostoevski refutes the philosophy of positivism Chernyshevski had set forth with such evangelical ardor in *What Is to Be Done?*

The nineteenth century, which witnessed the stupendous triumphs of science, delighted in the discovery of chaos, the creative value of the decadent, the connection between disease and inspiration. It was all part of "the romantic agony." The modern imagination is in many ways equally perverse in its efforts to give shape and form to the dementia of the age, which is the sickness of humanity. Objective and subjective reality, reason and madness, are brought together and made one. Antonin Artaud experimented with drugs which induce dreams and help to release images stored in the depths of the unconscious, even though he was aware that in doing so he was creating a literature of illness. He was fascinated by the art of weaving spells, the technique of evoking the euphoria of madness, the passions of paranoia. Words proved elusive and ineffectual since they distorted what he was seeking to convey. As Artaud wrote:

I suffer from a fearful mental disease. My ideas abandon me at every stage, from the mere fact of thought itself to the exterior phenomenon of its materialization in words. Words, the forms of sentences, inner directions of thoughts, the mind's simple reactions.—I am in constant pursuit of my intellectual being.[24]

As he labored to embody his haunting vision of the absolute, the landscape of reality disintegrated. Suicide or madness—these were the two alternatives open to the one who immersed himself in the destructive element.

Inside the locked cage of his disoriented mind, the writer pursues his difficult quest for the truth of reality. There is, as he sees it, no escape from the insanity of the world he is forced to live in. Life must go on regardless of how he feels, but the pressure of the dream that oppresses him does not let up. And it is the dream that shows him how equivocal are his relations to the external world. If Camus presents Caligula as the hero of the absurd, Artaud seizes on Heliogabulus as the exemplar of the absurd. Artaud, in embracing his madness, seeks like Baudelaire to transcend the limitations of the human.

The theme of madness, as it appears in literature from the time of Hamlet and Don Quixote to "the possessed" protagonists in Dostoevski's novels, the neurotic heroes of Strindberg and Kafka, the abnormal characters in Tennessee Williams's dramas, the drug-hallucinated and demented characters of the beat and hip writers—such a theme deserves a book all to itself.[25] This theme became a favorite one during the literary revolt of the expressionists, who rediscovered the world of the irrational and the grotesque. The literature of madness as divinest sense stems from the perception, deliberately heightened in the Pirandellian drama, that everything in experience is full of contradictions, so that it is impossible to say what is real. In *Henry IV*, Pirandello studies a case of insanity, pretended or real, and shows finally that madness is a relative state of being. The degree to which abnormality affects the mind and work of a writer is described in Sartre's book on Genet. Sartre pictures Genet as the victim of a persecution mania which he could not conquer.

Alienated from society, an "outsider" in his relation to the universe, the modern artist takes it upon himself to play the role of rebel, the enemy of mankind, the neurotic, the madman, the fool in Christ. His creative self is composed of a plurality of selves; he is frequently at war with himself; each of his chameleon selves gives a different interpretation of a reality that remains in the last analysis unknowable. He tries in his work to preserve the balance between the forces of life and death, illusion and reality, disease and health, madness and sanity. Though Freudianism made it possible for him to perceive the close relationship between art and disease, his attitude toward this aspect of Freudianism, and toward Freudianism as a whole, was decidedly ambivalent.[26] What he gleaned from Dostoevski and Nietzsche was the realization that disease could be a source of inspiration as well as suffering.

If art as disease paints a picture of the self as basically irrational, its vision of the world is equally irrational. It reveals a reality that reflects the alienated and disoriented condition of the mind. But it could prove fruitful only if the artist transfigured his dreams and dementias into the forms of art that would gather him, in Yeats's haunting phrase, into "the artifice of eternity." Those writers who were temperamentally opposed to the practice of art as disease could avail themselves of other more rewarding perspectives for contemplating the human condition.

We are no other than a moving row
Of magic shadow-shapes that come and go
  Round with the Sun-illumined Lantern held
In midnight by the Master of the Show;

But helpless Pieces of the game He plays
Upon this checker-board of nights and days;
  Hither and thither moves, and checks, and
    slays,
And one by one back in the closet lays.
                    RUBAIYAT OF OMAR KHAYYAM

1. ART AND LIFE AS A FORM OF PLAY

NUMEROUS BOOKS have been published on the way in which modern man envisages himself and his relation to society; he sees himself reflected as in a mirror in the eyes of others.[1] Other works of the imagination interpret man as an actor on the stage: the stage is the earth; society provides the scenario, the decor, the costumes, the lines of dialogue, though the plot is left largely indeterminate. The theme, too, though it is limited by the given nature of things, is protean in character. Another vastly fruitful metaphor regards life as a game to be played. Hemingway's heroes in *The Sun Also Rises* and *A Farewell to Arms* strive to live up to a code of honor, which demands that they must bear with grace, with a measure of courage and fortitude, the suffering that life inevitably imposes. Pirandello composed a play called *The Rules of the Game*. One of the rules requires that we assume a public role and act it out consistently. Each one, in conformity with his social and occupational role, performs a number of studied gestures and rehearsed attitudes. But when the public role bears little or no correspondence to the inner self, there is a split in consciousness. One French critic, in summing up Sartre's conception of the self in conflict, explains why man is often so willing to be poured into a socially prepared mold:

By identifying ourselves with an image which we construct mainly for others, we assume an easy role. Habit and routine rather than vanity motivate us; we choose the gestures appropriate to our profession and our position, and we repeat them automatically. The result is our mien, our self-assurance, our smugness—in brief, everything that has a part in the little game we play as if we were looking affably at ourselves in a mirror.[2]

All civilization, according to J. Huizinga in *Homo Ludens*, has its inception in and evolves as a form of play. Just as the child, in Wordsworth's "Ode on Intimations of Immortality," plays with some little plan and acts out his dream of human life, be it a wedding or a funeral, so does humanity engage in mimic play. The pervasiveness of play cannot be doubted. The presence of play introduces an aesthetic element and testifies to the power of mind in breaking down "the absolute determinism of the cosmos."[3] To interpret culture through the perspective of play is not a bit of rhetorical improvisation. The play instinct is universal. What distinguishes it is its spirit of freedom. For the time being the human player is removed from "real" life. Though this is all done in a mood of make-believe, the spirit of seriousness prevails. Indeed, games are often played with greater seriousness than "the real" business of life. The uniquely identifying feature of play is that it is conducted like a game, according to strictly defined rules. It imposes a humanly devised but binding order of procedure as in a ritual, with each move or gesture prescribed. Hence the close connection between play and aesthetics. In the latter as in the former, there are rules to be observed, conventions to be obeyed. Play, like religion, makes possible the coexistence of both belief and unbelief, the real and the make-believe.

The image of life as a game is closely linked with the image of life as a play, for a play, be it performed on the stage of society or in the closed, artificial world of the theater, also obeys a number of agreed-upon conventions. Thus we behold multiple perspectives in action, each of which, whether true or false, is psychologically and aesthetically advantageous; objectivity itself becomes a species of illusion. Ibsen, in *The Wild Duck*, in the *persona* of Doctor Relling, seems to support the will to illusion as a means of saving people from being destroyed by the feeling of self-contempt. As Doctor Relling says: "Take the saving lie from the average man and you take his happiness away, too."[4] Emotionally man is drawn to those fictions or vital lies that serve his needs. In this sense, then, psychology shapes cosmology.

There is nothing particularly new in the conception of art as a game or form of play, a device for viewing the painful spectacle of life through the lens of illusion. Nietzsche's affirmation of the principle of play as a universal aesthetic ideal was anticipated by Schiller in his *Letters on the Aesthetic Education of Man.* The metaphors designed to justify the endeavor of art are as richly varied as those that seek to justify the experiment of life: art as a sublimation of the sex instinct (Freud and Remy de Gourmont), art as an act of revenge against the chaos and absurdity of existence (Malraux), art as an imitation of the omnific creative act of God (Coleridge and the romantic poets), art as a vicarious quest for immortality (Otto Rank), art as a ritual of fantasy and illusion (Genet), art as symbolic action (Kenneth Burke), and so on. A number of modern writers have utilized this conception of art as a form of play. Purged of utilitarian aims, art, Gide held, is "innocent" as well as "gratuitous." "The ethic of art, in proportion as it is pure, is the ethic of play, of childhood, unadulterated by the notion of . . . the useful."[5]

But if life, like art, is a game and there are rules which must be followed, this does not mean that the individual invariably conforms to his role. He may refuse to obey, like the hunger artist, in Kafka's story, who fasts because he cannot help it, and he cannot help himself because he cannot find in life the kind of food he likes. As this "artist" wryly confesses: "If I had found it, believe me, I should have made no fuss and stuffed myself like you or anyone else."[6] The player may find the rules irksome and frustrating; he may refuse to accept a purely scientific interpretation of the universe; he may, in his revolt, reject all roles and rules. This was the motivation behind Alfred Jarry's 'Pataphysics, which marks the apotheosis of the absurd. A thoroughgoing nihilist in his protest, he took nothing seriously. He carried the myth of Sisyphus to its "logical" conclusion by deliberately drinking himself to death, but even as the prophet of 'Pataphysics and the author of *Ubu roi* he was playing a role.

Human behavior can thus be interpreted in terms of the game model. If human behavior is to be properly understood, the kind of game being played must be defined. Here is a sphere which is raised above the plane of morality and necessity. It lights up the face of the unknowable by its assumption that all is play. The game metaphor has a direct bearing on my theme of psychological relativism. As J. Huizinga eloquently declares, we know deep within us "that none of our pronouncements is absolutely conclusive. At that point, where our judgment begins to waver, the feeling that the world is serious after all wavers with it. Instead of the old saw 'All is vanity,' the more positive conclusion forces itself upon us that 'all is play.' "[7]

2. PIRANDELLO'S RELATIVITY OF VISION

Pirandello has been commonly bracketed with Shaw as a predominantly intellectual dramatist—an evaluation that Pirandello deplored since he felt it was not the truth about him and his work. But the intellectual taint is manifestly present in his dramas and fiction: the dialectic that enjoys the clash of opposites, the restless play of the mind which examines a problem simultaneously from a multiplicity of viewpoints, the awareness that we all live in private and incommensurable universes. He portrays characters who seek by means of the intellect to comprehend and thus control the suffering that life imposes, characters who, dwelling in their own subjective caves, entertain startlingly false or distorted conceptions of themselves and of the other person. Pirandello's recurrent theme stresses the universality of the human need for illusion. In interpreting the ongoing conflict between reality and illusion, he, like Cervantes, sees life as a stage, but he also pictures it in the image of a game that must be played according to the rules.

Pirandello differs from an intellectual dramatist like Shaw in that he is not concerned with social or political problems. A philosophical pessimist, he is not to be identified with any ideology. Though he offers no solutions (he believes there are none), he still feels that the mask of self-deception must be removed. Unlike Genet, he still contends it is possible for man to glimpse the naked truth about himself. He probes the innermost recesses of the self, convinced that he can thus arrive at a liberating psychological insight. His plays at least attempt to resolve the conflict between truth and illusion. In *Rules of the Game* (1918), he introduces a husband who plays the game according to his own rules. The husband prefers to take on the role of spectator, but he finds out at the end that he cannot remain detached. He had assumed that the one who wins the game of life is the one who keeps his feelings under strict control, but in his case things fail to work out according to plan.

Determined to keep on playing the game according to the rules, Leone, the husband, tells Guido, his wife's lover: "You must give up all hope, because only the absence of hope makes it impossible for you to compromise."[8] The way to win is to adopt the stoic's attitude, to drain the heart of all feeling. As Leone declares: "You must defend yourself from others and above all from yourself, from the pain which life inevitably inflicts on everyone."[9] This is the armor to wear as a protection against the slings and arrows of outrageous fortune. But if the soul must be emptied of all desire, all feeling, then, as Guido sensibly asks, what is left? What has the ethic of complete self-renunciation to offer? Leone's reply is characteristically Pirandellian in that it provides no answer but simply intensifies the problem of suffering. "The pleasure of not living for yourself, but of seeing how others live; not of acting for yourself, but of watching yourself in action—for those few years you're forced to exist."[10]

This is, in effect, the artist's confession of the strength he derives from his spectatorial role, as he watches with the unconcern of a god the contests being waged in the dust of the terrestrial arena. But it also reveals the damaging limitations imposed on him. The role denies him spontaneity of action and virtually cuts him off from the possibility of living his life. Here is a hero who has placed his intellect in full command of his feelings, and yet, despite all his stoical precepts, he continues to suffer. He tries to guide his life by the compass of reason and logic. It is the rationalist's trump card, and it is not good enough. He discovers that it is impossible to withdraw from life, impossible to insulate the self against suffering.

Unlike the dramatists of the absurd, Pirandello employs logically ordered plots to suggest the irrational element in life, the sudden eruption of the demonic and the perverse. His object is to expose the baffling contradictions of the human soul, the lies to which men and women cling in order to cover their shameful nakedness. Sincerity is an ideal few manage to attain. Lies, illusions, self-deception, duplicity: these are some of the moves they make as they endeavor to play the terribly complicated game of life. Head and heart, reason and emotion, cannot be brought into harmony, and the game is never won. The rules need to be precisely defined, but there is the rub: they are always, unpredictably, changing. The truth of reality, like the true nature of the self, is not to be known. When a character in another play, *To Clothe the Naked*, emphasizes the facts in the case, Ludovico, a novelist, ironically remarks: "My dear sir, the facts are what we assume them to be. In the life of the spirit there are no facts."[11] Each game establishes its own set of rules, and these must in turn be interpreted by the players, each of whom gives his own subjectively conditioned reading of the facts, when there are no facts in the life of the spirit. Pirandello's *dramatis personae* inhabit a world which is overshadowed by the principle of psychological relativism.

3. *THE GAME OF PHILOSOPHY*

Hermann Hesse, the artistic conscience of his race, has repeatedly portrayed the conflict between spirit and world, self and society, mind and reality, thought and truth, consciousness and reality. *Magister Ludi*, a philosophical fable, a utopian novel that seeks to discover the kind of ideal society to be established in the future, describes how a group of intellectuals organize the Castalian Order and devote themselves assiduously to the Bead Game. Their object is to synthesize all the arts and sciences. Absorbed in the life of meditation, the chosen ones find music and mathematics the noblest expression of the spirit of man.

The Bead Game is part of the curriculum of the Castalian Order; the rules of this game constitute a secret code, a language composed of the various arts and sciences, particularly music and mathematics. "The Bead Game is also a device that comprises the complete contents and values of our culture; it plays with them as . . . a painter may have toyed with the colours of his palette."[12] The adept in the Bead Game—and Joseph Knecht, the master, exemplifies the perfect model—utilizes everything that once went into the making of culture in all its ramifications. He plays with all the elements of the cosmic scheme as if they were so many instruments in an orchestra. Each player is free to form whatever combinations fall within the compass of his vision. Fundamentally, this spiritual movement is designed to effect a reconciliation between science and art or between science and religion.

Hesse is obviously composing a disguised philosophical allegory on the major conflicts of his age. Though we never get concrete examples of how the Bead Game is played except that it utilizes all the arts and sciences, relying particularly on abstract mathematical formulas and symbols, the presumption, of course, is that it is more than a game. It serves to support a new world and a new culture in the making. The game represents in symbolic form "the quest for perfection, a sublime alchemy, a self-reproach to the inherent spirit beyond all images and pluralities—and thus to God."[13] The goal sought is that of "realization," the discovery of the path from becoming to being.

The aim of the Castalian Order is to develop the opposition between conflicting themes, such as law and freedom, or individuality and community, but also to discover in them poles of a single unit. Each man should strive toward the binding of all opposites: logic and fantasy, the subjective and the objective, mathematics and music. Joseph Knecht, who dedicates himself with quasireligious ardor to the quest for knowledge, tells his master:

If only there were a doctrine—something in which everyone could believe! Everything is so contradictory, and there is no certainty: everything can be explained and then re-explained in the opposite manner. One can interpret the whole of world history as development and progress, and yet, on the other hand, one can just as well see in it nothing but decline and insanity. Is there no truth then, is there no true and valid doctrine?[14]

This sounds very much like a Pirandellian theme. Joseph Knecht struggles to overcome the psychological relativism which infects all of human knowledge and prevents man from arriving at absolute certainty. The master informs him that there is truth but no absolute doctrine that comprehends all phenomena. "The Godhead is in *yourself*, not in theories and in books. Truth must be lived, not taught."[15] This is the existential wisdom the neophyte must find out for himself.

After years of intensive study spent in the search for universality, Knecht finally comes to understand that each symbol of the Bead Game symbolizes the whole. In fact, this royal game provides a sacred language, a key to unlock the heart of the world. He endeavors to reconstruct the entire content of a Bead Game so that everything in it can be brought under a common denominator. Nevertheless, doubts begin to assail him. Could this universal language furnish a reliable guide in the kingdom of the spirit? What was it in reality but a game? Knecht, like Kierkegaard, is determined to rise above the aesthetic stage. Though as Magister, the leader of this community, he performs his duties with exemplary devotion, the split in his soul is not healed. He has not been able to achieve what he once declared was the ideal of the order: to reconcile the *vita activa* and the *vita contemplativa*. He has never lost his awareness of the world outside, of which Castalia is only a small part, and he is haunted by the transience of all things.

He gives up the utopian quest. There is no stopping point. He must start anew on his life's journey. It is not so much, he now perceives, a question of grasping the ultimate truth as of directly confronting reality. He is led closer to reality, which is ambiguous, closer to the truth, but this truth is ineffable. He is hungry "for reality, for tasks and deeds, and also for privation and suffering."[16] He will enter upon a new stage, even though he cannot rationally justify his choice. He will plunge into the world outside the Castalian Province, since he can no longer bear this feeling of isolation.

The life of the world as the Castalian saw it was something antiquated and inferior, a life of disorder and coarseness, of passions and vagaries in which there was nothing beautiful or desirable, but in actuality it was greater and richer than any description that I could possibly give as a Castalian. It was pregnant with future, history, efforts and eternal new beginnings; it was perhaps chaotic, but it was the homeland and the mother soil of all destinies, all revolts, all arts, all humanity; it had languages, people, states, cultures and had also engendered us Castalians, would see us all die and still go on.[17]

Castalia was, by comparison, a perfect but static world. Life, which perpetually renews itself, cannot be confined within the hermetic ritual of the Bead Game. There is no magic formula that can plumb the cosmic mystery. When Joseph Knecht perishes at the end, he has already left behind him the world of "fictions" and "games." Hesse, unlike Schopenhauer, is not convinced that the Idea can conquer the Will. A tragic writer, Hesse is saying like Pirandello that the answer to the riddle of life is not to be found. It is a dangerous temptation, this idea of playing the Bead Game by withdrawing from the world of mundane, human reality. The mystery abides all questions. Paradox pervades all of existence.

4. THE GAME OF THE ABSURD

If nonsense is actually a game played with words, the game is intended to keep the forces of the irrational at bay. If the game of nonsense is to be played effectively, the participants must, as in chess, adhere to the rules agreed upon. The chief aim of the game of nonsense is "to create a universe which will be logical and orderly, with separate units held together by a strict economy of relations, not subject to dream and disorder with its multiplications of relations and associations."[18] After Alice had pushed her way through the looking glass and reached the top of the little hill, she observed below her the country laid out curiously like a large chessboard. In a tone of delight she made the reassuring identification: "It's a great huge game of chess that's being played—all over the world—if this *is* the world at all."[19]

Lewis Carroll, as Dodgson, the university don, could play the game of life according to the prescribed rules of orthodoxy. Today the writers of the absurd, while likening life to a game one must play, consider the rules utterly ridiculous. As Roger Caillois says:

The game is ruined by the nihilist who denounces the rules as absurd and conventional, who refuses to play because the game is meaningless. His arguments are irrefutable. The game has no other but an intrinsic meaning. That is why its rules are imperative and absolute, beyond discussion. There is no reason for their being as they are, rather than otherwise.[20]

The analogy in this case does not entirely hold true, as the absurdist knows. The rules of games, since they are but games, can be changed by common consent, whereas the ground rules that apply to the game of life and death are unalterable. Even the proviso that the player is free to withdraw from the game if he so pleases does not, in this instance, carry much weight. Suicide is no solution. Sisyphus cannot renounce his own myth. The player is forced to continue the game, but he plays it in a mocking, ironic spirit.

Arthur Adamov's play, *Ping-Pong*, uses the image of a pinball machine to embody the hazards and caprices of fortune. The players are motivated by the desire to achieve success and gain power, though the game ends inevitably in death. The erratic behavior of the ball, the numbers that light up, the use of the left flipper, the possibility of achieving control, the jamming of the machine—all this makes for ingenious metaphoric implications. The epitome of amusement, the pinball machine offers "Action! Conflict! Participation!"[21] That is how Adamov represents the mysterious element of contingency. How can one learn to master the machine? Why does it regularly fall out of order?

In scene after fantastic scene, the metaphor of the gambling machine, dramatically sustained, provides an ambiguous but illuminating perspective for presenting the contradictions and ironic reversals of existence. Things are the opposite of what they seem, and yet events are interconnected, though still basically incomprehensible. One character remarks: "When the machine resists, don't be in such a hurry to accuse the machine. Ask yourselves if you haven't forgotten a wheel somewhere."[22] Let them cherish the hope of some future triumph. But the principle of the game is beginning to call forth widespread complaints: "You play, you try to understand, and you never know where you are, whether you're winning or losing, if you've still a chance or no chance at all."[23] And yet the desires of the players for novelty, suspense, and excitement are increasing. Life itself is one vast complicated pinball machine. At one point the Old Man, the owner of the Corporation manufacturing the machine, makes the confession that epitomizes the philosophy of the absurd: "What do I know about the machine? Nothing. I'm as lost as anyone else."[24]

Arthur, one of the principal characters, comes in with the news that he has worked out a new machine that he calls "On Earth As It Is In Heaven," a symbolic slogan that he is convinced sums up everything. "On the scoreboard," he says, "skaters move forward and airplanes crash."[25] He has disposed of the flipper; the balls roll and roll, and there is no way of telling whether or not the scoreboard lights up. The holes will provide for every imaginable possibility, since they offer both an opportunity for winning and a danger of losing. "You have to be afraid of them, and at the same time, to hope for them. You aim for them and if you miss them, maybe that's lucky. You aim for them and you make them, and maybe that's lucky, too. You can't tell."[26] Arthur is carried away by the magnificent originality of his invention, this *reductio ad absurdum*, especially by what he calls the return ball. No holes indicate when that will come back. "Because if you knew ahead of time what the chances were, then it would just be an ordinary pleasure, drudgery . . . all over again."[27] Arthur cries out in rage: "Naturally, you can't make the game last forever."[28]

The last scene, which drops the image of the pinball machine, also drives home the meaninglessness of the game of life. The two close friends in the play, Victor and Arthur, now old and white-haired, engage in playing ping-pong on a table divided into eight black and white squares. The game goes on, though they still have not decided what they are playing for. Victor decides to get rid of the squares. Then they remove the net, after which they throw their paddles away and play with their bare hands. The volleys grow wilder and wilder; the players make spectacular but clumsy leaps in returning the ball. Victor's movements are becoming progressively weaker. When Arthur hits the ball high, Victor leaps for it but falls to the floor, dead. The game is over.

Ping-Pong, like Samuel Beckett's *Endgame*, reveals the futility of the struggle; the game is ended, though the machine keeps on running. In Beckett's play the title seems to imply the death of the world. From the nihilist perspective, the universe is unjustifiable, and hence absurd. Adamov later abandoned the theater of the absurd and took to writing plays with a markedly social content. He decided to play the game according to rules that were close to the redemptive ideology expressed in Bertold Brecht's epic dramas. By shifting his perspective he arrived at a different version of reality.

> Remember that you are actor in a drama of
> such sort as the author chooses,—if short, then in
> a short one; if long, then in a long one. If it be
> his pleasure that you should enact a poor man, see
> that you act it well; or a cripple, or a ruler, or a
> private citizen. For this is your business, to act
> well the given part; but to choose it, belongs to
> another.   —EPICTETUS

> All the world's a stage,
> And all the men and women merely players:
> They have their exits and their entrances;
> And one man in his time plays many parts,
> His acts being seven ages.   —SHAKESPEARE

1. THE PROLOGUE

WHEREAS EPICTETUS counsels stoical resignation to another, a
higher, if mysterious, authority, Shakespeare's lines use the stage as
an arresting image, without introducing either an author or a director of the human drama. The metaphor, life is a stage, embodies
a form of perspectivism; it presupposes a metaphysical distrust of
the reality of the world. The self, enacting a particular role, inevitably colors the character of perceived reality. For Kierkegaard
subjectivity is truth. But self and world, the subjective and objective, are polar terms. No world, no self, but by the same token
no self implies no world. There is no such thing as a neutral environment. Some writers, as we shall see in the next chapter on
social realism, reverse the formula to read that "the objective"
world is primary. Lenin, as a dialetical materialist, contends that
"the human mind *reflects* the objectively real outer world."[1]

Ortega endeavors to reconcile object and consciousness and
fuse them in a phenomenological synthesis which does justice to
"the reality" of both. Reality constitutes a relationship; man is in
the world and apprehends the world; hence there is not one over-

arching Reality but an infinite number of realities, depending on the point of view from which each is seen. No two points of view, like no two individuals, are the same. There is, as Proust insisted, no reality subsisting independently of the observer. Einsteinian time and space necessitate the abandonment of the concept of absolute truth. Thus we get the philosophy of perspectivism or of absolute relativity, as some critics have called it. As Leon Livingstone points out:

Perspectivism is not, however, an abstract system for it derives from a relationship between the object—external reality—and a subject that is living and dynamic: man. As man changes, so changes his point of view and so changes the perspective that he views. Perspectivism is a theory that is valid for all times only because it can be adapted to all periods.[2]

Though perspectivism is valid at all times, it has become, thanks in part to the influence of Einsteinian relativity, a prominent, if not obsessive, feature of the modern literary consciousness. This is evident in the widespread conception of the world as a stage and of life as a play. But even within the purview of this key metaphor, apart from the pressure of other competing perspectives that seem equally "true," conflicts are bound to arise. Should one follow the advice of Epictetus and play to the best of his ability whatever role has been thrust upon him by the unknown author of the drama? Is the script, in fact, already prepared, so that the denouement and the ultimate ending are predetermined, though the "actor" cannot see that far ahead? Or is the stage metaphor to be construed differently, like a *commedia dell'arte*, in which the actor impersonating a given role is required to improvise for the occasion, so that "the actors became themselves their own authors"?[3] Even if the actors are aware of their histrionic role, how well do they identify themselves with it? Do they, in effect, *become* what they impersonate? But if that is the case, then who are they? This is the question that Sartre raises in one of his plays.

Kean, based on the play by Dumas, furnishes a witty and continuously interesting dramatic demonstration of the existentialist conception of the self. Who is Kean the actor? Does he have an essential self or is he merely the role that he temporarily assumes? The problem intrigues him. "Sometimes I wonder," he says, "if real emotions are not merely false emotions badly acted."[4] Everyone plays a part, badly or well. He knows that he strikes attitudes in everything he does. "Everything is provisional—I live from day to day in a fabulous imposture."[5] For him the stage has been reality and the world itself only a stage. "When the man himself is a sham, everything is a sham around him. Under a sham sun, the sham Kean cried the tale of his sham sufferings to his sham heart."[6] His whole life has been made up of gestures, one for every hour of his life. Now he is resolved to become authentically himself. "I will imitate the natural until it becomes second nature."[7] But when the play ends and he goes off to Washington, he is still playing a role.

Even the role a character chooses to adopt in life is an act that testifies to some freedom of choice on his part. If a man looks upon himself as constructed essentially like a machine, he will tend to behave like a machine and react to others as if they, too, were machines. This gives rise to a gigantic industrial society in which each robot carries out an automatic function. Or, like Dostoevski's underground man, he can refuse to play the game according to the rules. Most men, however, are compelled to play their assigned roles. The colossal technological apparatus, the *deus ex machina*, sucks them into its maw and exploits them as so many standardized units of productive energy. Economics is fate, according to this script, work is life, subjectivity is taboo. This results, as we shall see, in a vast social system of depersonalization.[8]

Those writers who assume the prophetic role of social planners (their views will be taken up in the section dealing with the utopian myth) have gone so far as to invoke the authority of science for legitimizing schemes that would induce human beings to recite their lines properly. Human happiness is to be organized in an "engineered" drama according to efficient principles of mechanical conditioning. The individual is to be so trained that he will spontaneously desire to do the "right" thing. Virtue will become a matter of habit. This is the perspective earnestly set forth in the didactic pseudonovel of ideas, *Walden Two*. As one enthusiastic supporter of the utopian vision declares:

The world of a stage play is not a world where unexpected events take place to which people must respond according to their lights; it is a world of strictly patterned activity. And of course one wants the actors to say their lines and make their gestures as flawlessly as possible: one wants the play to be performed: one does not want the actors to substitute words of their own or rearrange scenes or follow their whim. The trouble is that life is not a stage play: life is improvisation: at least, some of life is improvisation.[9]

This brings the problem of perspectivism sharply into focus: if reality is illusion and is ultimately unknowable, then life cannot be made to follow a preexisting script. The element of spontaneity, of the surprising, the fortuitous, and even the irrational, cannot be eliminated.

The artist, by virtue of living the life of the imagination, is an actor who gives himself, seriously or ironically, to his creative illusions. Precisely because he is an illusionist he does not live, he "plays" at the game of life, fashioning a symbolic version of reality that helps him in part to solve his problems. Nevertheless, like the decadent artists in Thomas Mann's stories, he feels frustrated because, unlike the good bourgeois, he does little more than contemplate his image in a mirror. "The artist's eye," Thomas Mann says, "has a mythical slant upon life, which makes it look like a farce, like a theatrical performance, like a Punch and Judy epic."[10]

The modern writer intuitively understands the dilemma faced by twentieth-century man in search of a lost self. In the manuscript of *La Mort Heureuse*, the first version of *The Stranger*, one character says: "There's only one question: to know one's own values. But to do this, you have to leave Socrates to one side. You know yourself you must act—and this does not mean that you can then say who you are. 'The Cult of the Self'—don't make me laugh, which self and which personality?"[11] According to this character, all the world's a stage, but he wonders if the life he and others are leading can be merely play-acting. For the actors in the drama of life do not know they are in a play; for them both the pain and the joy are real. If this is a game that is being played, then it is the most serious and exciting game there is. Camus's character wants to be a perfect actor. "I don't care about my personality and I'm not interested in cultivating it. I don't want to treat my life as an experiment, but to be what my life makes me. It is I who am the experiment, and it is life that forms and controls me."[12]

Each character in literature exists in his own right, enacts his own role. He is opposed, even within the autonomous world of art, by other characters who represent other points of view and different values. He may be in conflict with himself. The author is the composer and conductor who orchestrates all the points of view operative in his work. George T. Wright aptly sums up the dialectical process that governs a literary work. The writer

> relegates all the masks and all the surface action of the play to third-person position. The discretion with which he selects certain points of view for presentation, and his skill in arranging and controlling them, give to each in turn a deeper significance, for in any final analysis the meaning of each presented point of view . . . is formulable only with reference to the total hypostasis, the structure of meaning which the play as a whole represents: the playwright's voice, his deepest lyrical person, *his* point of view.[13]

Though Wright is using point of view in a technical literary sense, his remarks bear out the theme of perspectivism I have been expounding.

It is the writer, in short, who decides what he wants to reveal: how he is to employ plot, setting, dialogue, and masks. All of life is transformed into drama, into image or mask. It was Yeats who exalted "Mask and Image above the eighteenth-century logic."[14] For Yeats all happiness was linked with the energy that led one to assume the mask of some other self, so as to escape from or transcend the truth of reality. According to Valéry, it runs contrary to nature to see things as they are; that would mark the end of all hope. That is why nature puts on a bewildering variety of painted masks. The mind of man conjures up delightful visions of what is not. The dance, by breaking out of the bondage of the real, delivers the body from the entanglements of all that is false.[15] The stage makes it possible for the dramatist to go beyond any single view of reality; he experiments with all points of view. In the preface to his play, *The Immortals*, Yvan Goll declares: "We have forgotten that the primary symbol of the theatre is the mask."[16] The mask, embodying a principle that governs the drama, effects the transmutation of nonreality into fact.[17]

2. THE PLAY WITHIN A PLAY

A play is an imaginative product that nevertheless induces a willing suspension of disbelief. Though the characters who appear in it are only creatures in a play, they are invested with a reality all their own. They seem, indeed, to be imbued with independent life, as if they had usurped the creative function of the dramatist. In the modern theater, this is carried to a point where the nature of reality is brought into question. What Lionel Abel fittingly calls "metatheater" reflects a world that is shot through with illusion. As in expressionist drama, fantasy takes over and the shadowy symbols of the dream mediate the image of "the real." In the metaplay thus conceived, "life *must* be a dream and the *world* must be a stage."[18]

The Maids, *The Balcony*, and *The Blacks* are three fine examples of metatheater. Genet's characters act out, as in a play within a play,[19] the parts which their fantasy craves. Each one is in a sense the author of his own play. Genet brilliantly develops the theme that illusion is inescapable. Like O'Neill in *The Iceman Cometh*, he is seeking to demonstrate that illusions are indispensable to life, but there is a basic difference between his work and that of O'Neill. Whereas Genet's protagonists know that they are embracing illusion, O'Neill makes it clear that his alcoholic derelicts, who are unable to cope with reality, are better off nursing their pipe dreams.

What distinguishes Genet as a playwright is that he breaks down the barriers traditionally interposed between imagination and reality.[20] A homosexual and thief who discovered art as his means of deliverance, he is a perspectivist who beholds reality not as a fixed, empirical datum, but something to be shaped. Reality, as he portrays it, remains enigmatic and paradoxical. Struggling to transcend the limitations imposed by the life of reason, he strives to go beyond the artificially devised dualism of fact and fantasy, matter and mind, reality and dream. Genet is the savage iconoclast for whom truth is but false appearance. The vision he projects on the stage is no more to be relied on; it may be false too, but at least it serves a good purpose in exposing the collective conspiracy of falsehood. As Sartre observes in his monumental study, *Saint Genet*, Genet seeks through dreams and magical acts to fight against his fate and thus to free himself of a world that wants no part of him.

From the beginning of his literary career, Genet, like Ionesco, was concerned with the problem of determining what is reality, what is truth. Reality is full of disparate, deceptive, and conflicting elements. Even the imagination is impotent to recapture the truth of the past, for this past is reconstructed by the medium of memory and the flow of dream imagery. Like Gide and Rivière,

Genet is unsparing in his efforts to achieve full sincerity;[21] he is concerned, above all, to know himself. What fascinates him is the rich potentiality of the drama as ritual; it ceases to be an aesthetic spectacle and becomes a communion that involves both actors and audience. That is how Genet seeks to batter down the obstacles that prevent communication. He tears aside the veils of dissimulation society uses to cover up its festering vices.

The Maids ingeniously exploits the resources of the theater in order to challenge and subvert the conventional notions of what reality is. Genet builds up a facade that seems eminently plausible and then proceeds to tear it down and reveal what lies concealed behind it. The play deliberately employs a technique of mystification. It is extremely difficult, in following this dialectic of dissimulation, to disentangle the imaginary aspect from the real. If Genet is attracted to the theater by the element "of fake, of sham, of artificiality,"[22] he offers no version of what we can confidently accept as the truth.

The Maids is the story of two sisters in service, who hate their mistress and have betrayed her lover to the police. Fearing that their act of betrayal will be discovered, they attempt to poison madame. When that fails, one of them must die. Genet is showing, in this play, the identity of the real and the pretended. Life is a theater in which actors play their part, but it is hard to say who is lurking behind the role. As Sartre observes, in Genet's plays "every character must play the role of a character who plays a role."[23] Genet brings out the resentment felt by the two maids, the cruel fantasies of revenge they concoct. One way they act out their rebellion is by assuming the position of the detested mistress, living for a glorious and yet abject moment the dream of power, each one taking turns. *The Maids* brings out the extraordinary degree to which all men, in their shifting roles of subordination, play the staged game of duplicity.

3. THE PLAY OF ILLUSION AND REALITY

The high priest of the universe of fantasy, Genet breaks down the thin line which separates reality from illusion. Dream is reality and reality (so-called) is spun of the gossamer web of dreams. In *The Balcony* (1960), the demolition of reality takes place right at the start. The opening scene shows us a bishop, with his robe and mitre, who is only impersonating a bishop in a brothel. In real life he is a gas man. The Grand Balcony, for a price, provides studios with mirrors strategically placed where men can "realize" their most extravagant wishes. Madame Irma makes possible all the magnified images of self-glorification, the grandiose fulfillment of each wish, however perverse in character. Here, then, is not only a house of prostitution but a theater that stages plays in which the client is the actor and director as well as the dramatist. The outcasts of the world, the frustrated and the deviant and the deprived, can revenge themselves upon a power-structured, authoritarian society by living out their fantasies in a compulsive ritual of their own devising. Fantasy is the supreme myth-making power in the world.

Genet constructs a dramatic situation that far exceeds in complexity the effects Pirandello produced in *Six Characters in Search of an Author, Henry IV*, and *Rules of the Game*. When the bishop hears screams coming from some other studio, he wonders how much is faked and how much is genuine suffering. When he is alone, he stands in front of the mirror and gazes at his reflection holding the surplice. It is not ambition that prompts him to patronize this establishment; he wishes to be a bishop for the sake of the impression he creates. He is aware that in this house of synthetic illusions no evil is committed; it is all feigning. "The Devil makes believe. That's how one recognizes him. He's the great Actor. And that's why the Church has anathematized actors."[24] The technique Genet uses is a series of modulated and ironic perspectives; the make-believe that is embraced with passionate zeal is coupled with the knowledge that it is, after all, make-believe, just as the mirror reflects nothing but a dressed-up image.

Another patron, wearing the robe of a judge, wants the young beautiful woman who is chained to deny and then to admit her guilt. She must play her role as a model thief if he is to serve as a model judge. In another scene, a timid-looking man assumes the role of a conquering general on horseback. In the meantime, in the city outside the brothel, the rebels are making headway with their attack, flooding whole areas, blowing up dams. Irma is not at all troubled by the sound of firing or the reports of battles raging. She functions in a far more useful capacity by catering to the all-too-human need for illusion. As she says: "Everyone is free, and I'm not concerned with politics."[25]

Each character in *The Balcony* is defined by his obsession. Madame Irma never passes moral judgment on the peculiar behavior of her clients. She does not permit her girls to talk about their performance or to make fun of it. This is no joking matter. The comic touch spoils the effect. "A smile means doubt. The clients want sober ceremonies."[26] Irma, who has constructed an apparatus through which she can watch whatever is going on in every one of her furnished studios, is proud of the discreet professional atmosphere of her establishment. "The Grand Balcony has a worldwide reputation. It's the most artful, yet the most decent house of illusions."[27] In her house of consolation, "Comedy and Appearance remain pure, and the Revels intact."[28] Though these patrons, like the audience in the theater, know they are entering a house of illusions, they want the simulation to be "real." "They all want everything to be as true as possible. . . . Minus something indefinable, so that it won't be true."[29] Each individual customer brings his own scenario, completely thought out. Madame Irma's job is merely to furnish the actors and actresses, together with the props. No wonder she feels that the house takes on wings, ceases to be a bawdy house, and becomes a place of enchantment.

The Balcony offers a striking example of a play that endeavors to shatter theatrical illusion by showing that *all* is illusion. From her balcony, by means of her peep-hole system, Madame Irma sees that her customers betray no inclination to gain their ends in reality; their gratification comes from the knowledge that all this takes place in a realm of fantasy. They know they are not what they seem; it is only the illusion they crave. Genet focuses on the brothel as a microcosmic reflection of society. Only in Madame Irma's establishment does the true character of reality emerge. At the end of the play, Irma addresses the audience directly; she will prepare her costumes and studios for the following day, when business will go on as usual, regardless of which political regime is installed in power. "You must go home now, where everything— you can be quite sure—will be even falser than here."[30]

4. THE PLAY OF MASKS

The technique, in *The Blacks*, of presenting a play within a play, a fantasy within another framework of fantasy, carries still further Genet's art of perspectivism. The subtitle, "A Clown Show," suggests the flavor of irony and sardonic humor with which this dramatic experiment is spiced. What makes this approach to the race problem such an emotionally disturbing experience is that, instead of being concerned with ideas and theories, it probes deep into the subliminal regions of the mind. For once again Genet's

central theme is that fantasy rules the world. In dreams we behold
the image of our truth, even if it is a paradoxical truth.

In his foreword, Genet reveals the nature of the image that im-
pelled him to compose this play. "One evening an actor asked me
to write a play for an all-black cast. But what exactly is a black?
First of all, what's his color?"[31] Genet insists that *The Blacks* is intended for a white audience, but if it is ever produced before a
group that is entirely black, then a white person should be invited
to attend the performance and should be formally ushered to his
seat, preferably in the front row of the orchestra. "The actors will
play for him. A spotlight should be focused upon this symbolic
white throughout the performance."[32] If no white person can be
induced to attend, white masks should be distributed to the Negro
audience. If they refuse to wear them, then a dummy should be
used. This makes it clear that the symbolic action on the stage is
intended to draw the members of the audience into the passions of
the plot.

The Blacks presents the fantasies of revenge by a whole group,
all of whom are Negroes. The actors arrange themselves in two
bodies: those who by gesture, speech, and action will reveal the
fantasies cherished by the Negro race, and the masked Negroes
(representing the whites) who will portray what the Negroes
imagine is the white man's conception of the Negro people. The
Negroes act out the murder of a white woman, since this is what
the whites imagine Negroes are capable of. The fantasy of "projection" is powerfully built up: the alleged sexual potency of the
Negro,[33] the rape, the murder of the white woman. The clownish
element is exploited as a way of making this display of homicidal
hatred bearable to the whites in the audience. Genet stresses the
ceremonial aspects, reminding the spectators that this is only a
ritual performance, a play within a play that shuttles back and
forth between reality and illusion. Mirrors, mask, ritual, dream,
fantasy: these are the devices Genet uses to bring out the grotesque
contradictions of reality. The Negroes in this "clown show" see
themselves as the whites see them, but since the whites are Negroes
masked as whites, even this image is a reflection of their own tor-
mented consciousness of color.

Genet deliberately intensifies the clash of colors. The whites
are caricatures but so are the blacks, since they must "blacken"
themselves in order to satisfy the stereotyped preconceptions of
the white world. It is all part of the show that is being put on for

the benefit of the whites. Otherwise, as the audience is told by one of the actors, they could not bear the revelation of the truth. It is out of a sense of decency that the actors take the trouble "to make communication impossible. We shall increase the distance that separates us—a distance that is basic—by our pomp, our manners, our insolence—for we are also actors."[34] The ambiguity of the performance is thus multiplied. The Negroes on the stage are actors before the court that is supposed to be white but is actually black and before an audience that is white. They are also actors who, when they leave the stage, must play a part in the white world they live in. On stage or off stage they must wear a mask.

When the Negroes go through the ritual of mourning for the dead woman by sitting around the catafalque and smoking, the governor, who is "white," believes that they are preparing, like cannibals in the jungle, to cook her body and eat it. The missionary assures the queen that she is safe. "Have confidence, Majesty, God is white."[35] He made possible the glory that was Greece. "For two thousand years God has been white. He eats on a white tablecloth. He wipes his white mouth with a white napkin."[36] This derision of the whites, this obsession with color, is characteristic of a minority race that is despised because it is black.[37] The play gives us abundant clues to Genet's underlying strategy: not only is he fashioning a fantasy of hatred, he is also giving utterance to the sheer poetry of hatred.

In a world ruled by whites, the Negro comes to detest his own color, to hate his ancestral past in Africa, and to hate all those who compel him to indulge in this masochistic orgy of hatred. If the Negroes are children, as the whites maintain, then there is nothing left for them to do but to live up to their assigned role by exploiting the resources of the theater. By virtue of being Negroes, they are forced to become performers on a stage. And yet, while performing the tragicomedy of their race, they cease to be Negroes; the fantasy liberates them from their role even as they assume it. "Now, this evening—but this evening only—we cease to be performers, since we are Negroes. On this stage, we're like guilty prisoners who play at being guilty."[38]

The play as a whole is made up of a series of assumed roles. We witness the fantasy of the extermination of the whites who had come to Africa to rule. The "white" queen is told: "To you, black was the color of priests and undertakers and orphans. But everything is changing. Whatever is gentle and kind and good and tender will be black. Milk will be black, sugar, rice, the sky, doves, hope, will be black."[39] The white race is exhausted and is slated for extinction, a prophecy Julius E. Lips confirms in his anthropological study, *The Savage Hits Back*. In all this ritualized make-believe there shines forth a baleful, frightening truth. The Negro woman who played the part of the white queen declares: "We masked our faces in order to live the loathsome life of the Whites and at the same time to help you sink into shame."[40] They must murder the whites, but for that they require no knives or guns. Since they are actors, the massacre they carry out will be lyrical. The symbolic destruction of the white race is clownishly effected. The final words uttered are instinct with menace: "We are what they want us to be. We shall therefore be it to the very end."[41]

5. THE SUMMING UP

The dialectic of illusion, the perspective of the dream, the technique of enclosing a play within a play, the use of masks and fantasy—all this is rendered dramatically convincing by the implied premise that they constitute, after all, a reflection of reality and an impassioned protest against that reality. Even Genet, the master magician of the show, directs his ritual of make-believe against the wielders of power by disclosing that they are themselves, like the revolutionists in *The Balcony*, prisoners of a myth. *The Maids*, equally with *The Balcony*, carries distinct social overtones. In *The Blacks* the racial protest comes through with overwhelming force. Once the boundaries that separate reality from fantasy break down, the "illusion" enacted by the Negro actors unmasks the hideous "truth" of social reality.

Genet and Brecht—the two dramatists are poles apart and yet their plays possess significant points of resemblance. Genet makes his audience believe they are in a theater and the actors are only playing a part. He does this in order to heighten the effect of illusion so that the spectators will become involved in the action on the stage. Illusion thus becomes reality. That is how values can be inverted, convictions undermined, the "truth" of reality challenged and blown apart. Genet experiments with the technique of "alienation," though, unlike Brecht, he does not use it for political ends. The various methods he uses to achieve alienating effects are designed to reinforce the impression that the spectacle on the stage is of illusion all compact. What we get is a highly concentrated form of symbolic theater which is "revolutionary" in its impact without being in the slightest degree ideological. Brecht, however, tries to use the theater to defeat the enchantment that is the triumph of art; he tries to eliminate or greatly reduce "the illusion" that the stage is capable of generating. His technique of alienation differs from Genet's dramaturgy in that he is seeking to demonstrate how man can master the world of reality. I shall deal in the next chapter with the counterperspective of social realism.

PART TWO / COUNTERPERSPECTIVE

1. WHAT IS TO BE DONE?

JUST AS Vladimar Mayakovsky demanded a new, dynamic kind
of poetry, so the radical Russian critics of the nineteenth century
had agitated in favor of an aesthetic philosophy that stressed the
primary importance of social reality. Mayakovsky wanted his
lyrics to capture "the roar of factories and laboratories."[1] As he
declares in one of his propagandistic poems, he wants his "output"
assigned "as part of the State."[2] More militantly he desires the pen
to produce what would be the equivalent of iron in industry. This
apotheosis of materialism, machinery, and communism represents
the culmination of an ideological process that goes back in time to
the forerunners of the Russian Revolution: Belinsky, Chernyshevski, Pisarev, Dobrolyubov, Marx, and Engels. Here is poetry
which, like socialist realism in fiction, strains to embody the materialist conception of history and life.

The materialist believes that "reality"—and by that he means
the world as revealed by the scientific method—is the ground of
all value, the touchstone of truth, not to be compared to the false
dreams of the imagination or the vagaries of subjectivity. Like

Chernyshevski and Pisarev, Vissarion Grigorievich Belinsky (1811-48) emphasized the fundamental importance of *reality*: the visible, material world of nature that man is destined to conquer. He confidently affirmed this article of faith in the face of those skeptics who despaired of attaining "the truth." Literature, like art, serves one constructive aim and function: to reproduce the world outside, though it is not of course to be a carbon copy; the creative imagination must not only render the truth of reality but also interpret and evaluate it. The tendentious element in Belinsky's aesthetic outlook is evident in his rejection of those writers who simply viewed the world as if from a great height, not implicating themselves in the scene they were describing. By calling for a change of heart or by postulating a nonexistent realm of spirit, they were guilty of shirking their social responsibility. Objectivity of this kind is reprehensible. The writer must take sides.[3]

Chernyshevski, too, consistently strikes this note as both critic and novelist. Fictitious realities are only "copies of what is provided by the phenomena of reality."[4] Human subjectivity is opposed by a world that refuses to gratify its wishes. Only by acting in conformity with the laws of nature and in harmony with his own being can man succeed in transforming reality and bringing it closer to the heart's desire. It is futile to strive for the realization of aims that are impossible of attainment. Hence the dreams of the imagination are to be scrapped; only those desires are to be indulged which have their roots in reality. That is the identifying mark of the rational man.

In a review of his own dissertation for the degree of master of arts, *The Aesthetic Relation of Art to Reality* (1855), Chernyshevski insists that the artist must faithfully serve the cause of the *real*. There is no question in his mind as to what constitutes "the real" as opposed to the a priori, the metaphysical, the never-never land of wishful thinking. Chernyshevski, like Belinsky, would have aesthetics derive its basic principles and methods from the sciences. The metaphysical systems of the past must be discarded in favor of a philosophy of aesthetics that is more in keeping "with science's new conceptions of nature and human life."[5] A powerful polemicist of the 1860s, Chernyshevski believed devoutly in science as the source and guarantee of truth. Spiritual abstractions were no longer necessary in explaining how the mind works. The human organism is but the product of chemical forces in interaction. Man is a part of nature. There are no absolutes; everything on earth is shaped by the influence of time, place, and circumstance. Chernyshevski hammers home his thesis that art must grow directly out of reality as determined by scientific coordinates.

His novel, *What Is to Be Done?*, which he wrote while he was in prison, presents a "positive" hero, a prerevolutionary martyr. It became the Bible of the Russian "nihilists," a group of men who sought to live according to the principles of positivism, without curbing the legitimate demands of the ego. The declared aim of the group was to live rationally, to base all interpretations of reality on experimental knowledge. Opposed to idealism in the field of aesthetics, Chernyshevski composed this novel in order to promulgate his naturalistic system of ethics and his belief that art must be put in its place as a servant of reality.

What Is to Be Done? is a novel only by semantic stretching of the term. It is actually a solemn tract on the theme of rationalism and the scientific meaning of reality. As a historical document, however, it is of considerable value for my purpose in studying the emergence of a militant counterperspective. What it brought home to many Russian intellectuals in the second half of the nineteenth century was the glorious gospel, as it then seemed, of materialism vindicated, of reason deified. It was not abstract reason that Chernyshevski apotheosized but reason harnessed to the motor of science. This faith in reason was coupled with the naïve assumption that all human behavior was dictated by the motive of self-interest. The hero, Lopukhóv, is, like Bazarov in *Fathers and Sons*, contemptuous of ideals, sentimentality, and metaphysical speculation.

The novel itself is concerned for the most part with the vexed problem of marriage and the lack of freedom from which the Russian woman then suffered. It gives expression to Fourierist ideas on the establishment of phalansteries and the pragmatic possibilities of changing human nature. It begins with the reported suicide of Lopukhóv, who is supposed to have blown his brains out in order to leave Vera Pavlovna, the new emancipated woman, free to live with the man she truly loves. In his preface, Chernyshevski frankly acknowledges that though he deals with the theme of love and provides the traditional fictional elements of suspense, he is really interested in disclosing "the truth"; he therefore warns the reader that he will find in this story "neither talent nor art, only the truth."[6]

The apostle of the religion of science, Lopukhóv experiments on frogs and explores the mystery of the nervous system. He confides to Vera his views on the inequality of women, his wish to remove the curse of poverty. He hopes that a time will come when men and women may be united in bonds of true friendship. This is part of Chernyshevski's intention: to beat the drum resoundingly in behalf of the ideal of equality and social justice and the sovereign cure to be effected by the application of the scientific method. Lopukhóv teaches Vera, his willing disciple, the meaning of enlightened self-interest. Everything, even the noblest aspirations, can be reduced to that. Lopukhóv is glad when Vera points out that this psychology seems lacking in human warmth; the mind should judge all matters coolly. It is precisely because science has no use for the passion flowers of poetry that it can produce such technological miracles.

Lopukhóv continues to harp on the theme that whatever pressures are brought to bear on a man, in the last analysis it is the law of self-interest that determines his behavior; there is no such thing as freedom of the will. There is no use berating the criminal for his behavior, for he cannot help being what he is. When Lopukhóv helps Vera free herself from the tyranny of her mother, he persuades himself that he is doing so not out of love for the girl or because she is beautiful. Of course not! They will live together as friends, in two separate rooms, so that each will be able to enjoy to the full the privilege of freedom and privacy. This is the way the new man and the new woman plan their life of love. Lopukhóv, "instead of cherishing lofty and poetic dreams . . . was absorbed by such dreams of love as are in harmony with the gross nature of materialism."[7] Faithful to his rational philosophy, he enters into this relationship with the firm conviction that he loves no one but himself.

Once this socialist marriage of true minds is consummated, Vera conceives the plan of establishing a dressmaker's shop on a cooperative basis. Then Chernyshevski hints of Vera's awakening passion for Kirsanov, Lopukhóv's close friend. But even in the unraveling of this romantic love knot, Chernyshevski makes rationalism triumph and shows egotism to be the dominant motivating force in human behavior. If people are to live in accordance with socialist principles, then love and marriage must come under the law of reason. A "true believer," Chernyshevski explains everything in terms of his utilitarian psychology, even Lopukhóv's decision to withdraw from the scene by a pretended act of suicide.

We are introduced to another character, Rakhmetov, who personifies the saint of rationalism, the new man who lives ascetically (though he will not sacrifice his cigar!) in accordance with a system of what he believes to be "true" principles of conduct. Chernyshevski, who repeatedly interrupts the course of the narrative to present his own commentary, declares that the first prerequisite of art is "to so represent objects that the reader may conceive of them as they really are."[8] He is not, he assures us, idealizing the "new people" of his generation, he is describing them as they are.

It was this portrait of the revolutionary optimist that infuriated Dostoevski. Whatever Chernyshevski lauded—the triumph of reason, the ideal of establishing a scientifically managed utopian society—was anathema to Dostoevski. The first part of *Notes from Underground*, published in 1864, a year after the appearance of Chernyshevski's novel, is a vigorous frontal assault on the central thesis of scientific rationalism, the belief that human nature could be controlled for its own good and that reason should be the controlling force in life.[9] Through the voice of his antihero, Dostoevski boldly challenges the premise that man primarily seeks pleasure and well-being. These dazzling visions of a materialist paradise run counter to the fundamental needs of human nature. Not all the comforts and conveniences in the world, according to Dostoevski, can serve to satisfy the human soul.

In fashioning this image of the positive hero, the radical critics in Russia tended on the whole to make character "a function of doctrine."[10] Literature was to be used as a vehicle of ideological enlightenment and social reform. Art, according to this categorical demand, was designed not merely to portray the world of reality but to change it. This critical approach was taken over by a number of Marxist writers in the twentieth century. Lukacs approves of the radical critics of nineteenth-century Russia who argued "that every work of art must be regarded as a product of the social struggle."[11] Lukacs, like Chernyshevski, carries on the tradition that literature reflects social reality. Literary evolution is a function of social evolution. Lukacs praises Gorki for his work as a poet of the class conflict; here is a proletarian humanist who is an optimist without illusions. "Illusions veil reality and the lives of those who harbour illusions are not real lives, but only lives of illusions or of lost illusions."[12]

I shall not trace developments in the art of socialist realism in Russia after the Revolution. One historian of Soviet literature declares: "A return to the full precepts of 'socialist realism' . . . now seems no longer possible."[13] Instead I shall analyze the social perspective as it is incorporated in the work of Bertold Brecht, a dramatist of international importance.

2. *THE SOCIAL PERSPECTIVE IN BERTOLD BRECHT*

It is certainly true that the image of life which literature projects is bound in some measure to reflect the life of society. Every character in literature, however introverted or negative, has been shaped in part by the social forces and cultural compulsions of his age.[14] While every hero, even the rebel whom Lautréamont presents in *Maldoror,* is in a sense the product of his milieu, what identifies him are precisely those qualities which accentuate his individuality and uniqueness. The same land that gave rise to the bitter realism of Gorky and later to his revolutionary romanticism also produced the nihilistic despair of Andreyev. During the stormy period between 1885 and 1898, the decadents in France adopted a characteristically hostile attitude toward society, especially the ruling middle class, but their revolt was motivated by personal rather than social reasons. "Des Esseintes' cry of revolt at the end of *A Rebours,* 'So crumble away society! Perish old world!' is nothing more than the curse of desolate pessimism and ennui; it is not social but personal."[15]

The psychological state of alienation, so prevalent in the literature of our time, has little to do with socioeconomic conditions or the pressures of politics. Man today feels alienated because he sees himself as a passive victim of external forces; everything in the world—nature, people, his own self—is alien to him.[16] The writer who accepts the Marxist system of eschatology is convinced that the abolition of the capitalist method of production and the ultimate establishment of the classless society will bring this wretched condition of alienation to an end.

Writers of this persuasion confidently assume that they know beforehand what "reality" is. Bound by the constraining logic of their metaphysical perspective, they are committed to only one kind of literature: social realism. Later, under Soviet auspices, this becomes socialist realism. Society for them becomes the all-inclusive metaphor; literature is supposed to be a symbolic preparation for the life of revolutionary action. The aim of literature is not only to reflect social reality truthfully; it must also be agitational, constructive, and optimistic in content. Unlike bourgeois writers, Marxist-oriented writers do not communicate a *Welt-anschauung* that is steeped in pessimism. They can predict fairly accurately the course of historical development, and they know that the emergent future is bright with promise. Georg Lukacs writes prophetically:

> Those who have arrived at such knowledge know, in spite of all temporary darkness, both whence we have come and where we are going. And those who know this find the world changed in their eyes: they see purposeful development where formerly only a blind, senseless confusion surrounded them.[17]

Though Marxism cannot divine each detail of the dialectical process, it can chart the general direction in which history is steadily and inevitably moving. "The final certainty it affords consists in the assurance that the development of mankind does not and cannot finally lead to nothing and nowhere."[18]

This is clearly a declaration of teleological faith. This type of messianic preachment disguised as dialectical materialism commits the writer to a form of literary realism that stresses types rather than individuals. It is this dogmatic assurance that "reality" can be scientifically or dialectically determined which culminates in an ideologically distorted and untenable aesthetic. Everything is reduced to politics. Literature is to be more than an imaginative reflection of socioeconomic conditions; it is to be transformed into a potent weapon. As far as the theoreticians in Soviet Russia were concerned, the revolutionary hero should be animated by the ideal of changing what is into what should be. During the 1920s, the honeymoon period of the Revolution, mechanical Marxism prevailed in the psychological study of man. He was looked upon as a machine; concepts like "consciousness" and "will" were eliminated since they smacked of subjectivism and idealism.[19]

These, roughly summed up, are some of the ideological presuppositions that the writer as convinced Marxist tends in general to accept. Like Chernyshevski, Bertold Brecht firmly believed, as he stated in "A Short Organum for the Theatre," that it is possible "to compile an aesthetic of the exact sciences."[20] The "new" scientific method Brecht adopted is that of dialectical materialism, a philosophy that combines doubt and faith, skepticism and affirmation. If Brecht applied the dialectic of doubt boldly to his "epic theater," it was because it could be used effectively to undermine vested "truths." If man was to control his physical and social environment, then he must master the technique of empirical observation. He must challenge every belief, take nothing for granted. Hence Brecht exalted Promethean man, the hero who proceeds to change the world. But what saves his plays from the taint of dogmatism is his insistence on the power of skepticism. He wrote a poem called "In Praise of Doubt," which describes the poor man who is told

> That this world is the best of all possible worlds and that the leak
> In his attic roof was put there by God himself.
> Really, it is difficult for him
> To query this world.[21]

Brecht persisted in using the stage as a means of querying this world.

Though Brecht explicitly defines his purpose in experimenting with what he called "epic theater," the way in which his epic theater actually functions is highly complex. It involves a theory of action, an underlying philosophy of aesthetics, an ethical and propagandistic conception of the dramatic form. Brecht's technique of "alienation" was concerned primarily with the problem of using the theater as a didactic instrument that he hoped would help to change the world by working directly on the minds of the audience. This technique involves a whole repertory of interrelated elements. The actor must not sink himself in his role to a point where he loses his identity. Like expressionist drama, the epic theater relies on song, music, lighting, scenic design, dance, and choral interludes to enrich its presentation, comment on the structure of "the plot," and support its message. What we get is a radically revised dramaturgy that is meant to vitalize the theater by associating it closely with the turmoil of events, the storm of politics, the impact of economic conflict, and the class war. In practice, however, Brecht did not subordinate his epic theater to the requirements of socialist realism.[22] If, on the one hand, he shattered the "illusionist" theory of the theater, he was able, on the other, to make full use of antirealist techniques and to rebel against the arid cult of verisimilitude.

Brecht, the dramatist who is also a poet, cannot be summed up in a formula. Despite his professed aim of breaking down the emotional identification of the spectators with what they beheld acted out on the stage, his plays have survived because of their undeniable power to arouse the emotions of the audience. The illusion his plays build up is so intense that the audience is able to adjust itself even to the use of a narrator. Empathy is not the same thing as "illusion." There can be no question, however, that after his conversion to communism Brecht wished to impregnate his plays with revolutionary motifs. He wanted the workers to accept the challenge of transforming society.

Once he embraced the communist faith, Brecht's conception of reality, society, and the self underwent a profound change. He adopted a perspectivism which in his epic dramas is intended to inspire the audience with the feeling that the social world can be changed. The theater must expose the working of the social machine. The Brechtian theater is thus devoted to the task of showing that the structure of society is not sacrosanct and immutable but, like all things in every period of time, subject to change. Society and its institutions decisively affect the character of man, but history, since it is man-made, can be brought under human control.

The technique Brecht utilized in his plays illustrates the importance he attached to the problem of change. He would alienate or estrange—that is, break up and present in a different light—those institutional arrangements which seem natural to the audience; he would make these forces in the social universe, now taken for granted, seem "strange" by presenting them from different perspectives. Tradition, custom, precedent, use, and wont—these are not immovable obstacles, just as society is not an unassailable establishment. The technique of alienation, Brecht explains,

allows the theatre to make use in its representations of the new social scientific method known as dialectical materialism. In order to unearth society's laws of motion this method treats social situations as processes, and traces out all their inconsistencies. It regards nothing as existing except in so far as it changes, in other words is in disharmony with itself. This also goes for those human feelings, opinions, and attitudes through which at any time the form of men's life together finds its expression.[23]

This is Brecht's aesthetic version of Marxist relativism, which is nevertheless an aesthetic of commitment. Since nobody can possibly divorce himself from the human race, every orientation is necessarily ideological, opposed to or in favor of the entrenched socioeconomic system. "Thus for art to be 'unpolitical' means only to ally itself with the 'ruling' group."[24] The enemy of wishful thinking and romantic illusions, Brecht wrote dramas that presented a schematic, grossly simplified version of reality.

3. THE EARLY BRECHT

The early Brecht, however, turns out to be not only an expressionist but a tragic writer who voices a nihilistic metaphysic. He is aware of the indescribable beauty of nature but also of its cruel indifference to the needs of mankind. In *Baal*, he draws an unforgettable portrait of the alienated poet-protagonist who savagely opposes a society based on the cash nexus. The hero, who is named Baal,[25] exposes the worst features of our mercantile civilization: its callousness, its cupidity, its crass disregard for human suffering. Such a society, governed by the bourgeoisie and dominated by sordidly materialistic values, epitomizes the spirit of boredom. One can be cured of this deadly malaise in only one way: by releasing the spontaneous life of instinct, which is amoral in its expression. More important than money or success is the fulfillment of sensuality outside the bonds of marriage. Baal indulges orgiastically in sex not only because he is endowed with a superabundance of vital energy but because his imagination makes him realize there is nothing else on earth worth living for; he is a nihilist in his perception that life is destructive. The universe is totally without meaning and sex is one way of shutting out that frightening knowledge. *Baal* pictures a world that is red in tooth and claw; life feeds on life, but the earth is beautiful. Baal is the anarchistic rebel who cannot be held in check by Christian ethics; he lives in immediacy, he obeys his desires, he believes in no system of salvation. The earth is one of the smaller planets revolving in a sky that is always black; death comes and "everything goes on as before."[26] Death is freedom; nothing lasts, not even in the grave. "The worms inflate themselves. Putrefaction crawls toward us."[27] It is a curse to be thrust into this world, where men vainly seek "the country where there's a better life."[28] Baal is a fighter, but his battle is waged not against society but against the supreme enemy, death.

The Swamp, first produced in 1922, four years after *Baal*, exposes the vulpine greed of men in an insanely competitive society. The action of the play takes place in Chicago in the year 1912. This is the "civilized" jungle Brecht undertakes to explore. George

Garga, a worker in a bookstore, knows the misery of poverty and feels the economic noose drawn tighter and tighter around the necks of the exploited masses. He is filled with a bitter resentment against his fate, but he continues to cling to his integrity. When he is fired from his job, his rage against this iniquitous society breaks out in full force. Like Baal, he sees that it is composed of hypocrites, liars, misers, greedy merchants, but unlike Baal he tries to make his protest felt. His aggressive instincts are brought into play. In a world ruled viciously by the profit motive there is no room for love; the only effective weapon to be used is that of hatred and hostility.

The underlying theme that informs Brecht's later plays is present here in the germ. The socioeconomic perspective that Brecht is struggling to formulate is implicit in the metaphysical boxing match, as it were, between Garga and Shlink. The latter proposes an experiment: he will turn his lumber business and his house over to Garga, who feels that he is tied hand and foot. Everything in the world, including the life of man, is mortgaged for a price. Misery is inescapable. Things are always getting worse. Garga gives utterances to Brecht's despair over the unregenerate condition of man. "The bottoms are dropping out. The scum shows itself, but its desires are weak."[29] Man possesses many possibilities; he "is destroyed by trivial causes alone."[30]

Shlink and Garga are bound together by their metaphysical compact. Shlink is a realist who knows that "the end is not the goal, the last episode is not more important than any other."[31] Understanding between men under the present social order is out of the question; each one is isolate and unable to communicate. Men are descended from the apes. Garga, like Baal, suffers from a devouring pessimism. His craving for power and conquest is all an idle dream, but if that is so he will choose a life of pleasure. In reacting against a form of existence infected by the dry rot of boredom, he betrays the cause of idealism. He has reached a stage of defeatism where spiritual values are utterly stripped of significance. "It is not important to be the stronger one," he says, "but to be the living one."[32] It is this attitude of despair that Brecht will later transform into an ethic of defiance.

Saint Joan of the Stockyards describes the experience of a girl who joins the Salvation Army but learns to her cost that it is the capitalist system which is the root of all evil. The scene, as in *The*

Swamp, is laid in Chicago, in the stockyards. Joan, at the head of her shock troops, brings the message of Christian redemption. She is making her first descent into the inferno of proletarian misery. What a crazy pattern of ordered disorder capitalism presents: humanity dehumanized, industrial unrest and strife, "a world like a slaughterhouse."[33] Joan has come to prevent, if she can, the threatened outbreak of violence by preaching the gospel of God to the benighted masses; she will make God's word effectual in "real" life. Here, as in Shaw's *Major Barbara*, are the soldiers of the Lord marching to the rescue, offering the kingdom of heaven to all who will enter.

What afflicts these wretched workers is not poverty but their blindness to higher things. Force, far from solving their problem, will only result in chaos. Mauler, the meat king, whom Joan attempts to convert (again we have a contest, this time between Christ and Mammon), has no pity for mankind. Like Garga, he is convinced that man is evil. The nature of man must be changed before the disjointed world can be set aright. Joan, however, discovers that the poor are not base; it is the evil of poverty that drags them down. The packers, for their part, argue that it is impossible to do anything to alter economic law. Gradually Joan becomes aware of the cutthroat competition that goes on, the way in which all altruistic impulses are stifled. How can morality ever assert itself when the poor are deprived of everything? In this world, as Brecht portrays it, each man tramples brutally on the face of his competitor in order to make a profit.

The crisis comes to a head. The men are without work and their mutinous discontent is increasing dangerously. They are rousing their spirit to rebel against these intolerable conditions. The workers, in chorus, sing their song of defiance, proclaim their faith in ultimate victory. They are learning how to fight the common enemy. Joan, in her effort to help the people, has only succeeded in harming them. No talk of the spirit or appeals for the merciful intercession of God can solve the problem of the suffering masses. Brecht leaves the audience in no uncertainty as to his message when Joan in her dying moments cries out:

> Oh, let nothing be counted good, however helpful it may seem,
> And nothing considered honorable except that
> Which will change this world once for all: that's what it needs.[34]

4. ETHICAL RELATIVISM AND THE EPIC DRAMA

Beginning in 1928, Brecht turned his talent to the writing of didactic plays designed to drive home a collectivistic thesis. The individual must subordinate himself to the will of the social body, the imperative of history. *The Measures Taken* (1930) offers an excellent example of ethical relativism. One critic calls it "the one classic tragedy of communism which world literature possesses."[35] It is scarcely a tragedy in the sense in which we commonly use the term. It presents a problem of conscience. It illustrates the close connection that exists between a writer's purpose—in this case communist propaganda—and the form he employs. *The Measures Taken* shows little interest in individualized characters; the four agitators are interchangeable; they have no names, their identity is unimportant, only the cause which they serve is important. Here is a play that presents a Marxist conception of morality.

Brecht wants to show why a devoted, idealistic comrade has to be shot and thrown into a lime pit so that no trace of his body will be found. The four agitators address the audience directly, explaining that the young comrade often did the right thing for the wrong reason. In employing the wrong means, he endangered the movement, even though his motives were idealistic. "The sight of injustice drove me into the ranks of the fighters. Man must help man. I am for freedom. I believe in humanity. And I am for the measures taken by the Communist party which fights for the classless society against exploitation and ignorance."[36] This sets the tone of the play and suggests the conflict to be worked out between humanitarian sentiment and the exigencies of the class struggle. The situations are arranged not for their dramatic but their exemplary value.

Each of the scenes demonstrates the dangers the party agent must face, the sacrifice of self he is required to make. In order to carry out their assignment in Mukden among the Chinese workers, the four agitators must lose their identity. They must not be seen; the authorities are suspicious. If one of them is wounded, he must not be found alive; even his dead body must be disposed of. As the Leader tells them: "Then you are yourselves no longer. . . . One and all of you are nameless and motherless, blank pages on which the revolution writes its instructions."[37] The Leader gives them masks, which they put on. They must be unknown workers, Chinese at all times, not only in appearance but even in thought and in sleep. The Young Comrade, by agreeing to this sacrifice of his identity, is saying "yes to the revolutionizing of the world."[38]

Lest the meaning of the parable should possibly be misinterpreted, the Control Chorus takes up the burden of the dialectical theme:

> Who fights for Communism must be able to fight, and not to fight; to speak the truth and not to speak the truth; to perform services and not to perform services; keep promises and not keep promises; to go into danger and to keep out of danger; to be recognizable and not to be recognizable. Who fights for Communism has only one of all the virtues: that he fights for Communism.[39]

This affords a good illustration of Marxist morality in action. The end justifies the means. It necessitates duplicity, deception, disguise, lying, but the revolutionary victory, when it is achieved, will set all things right. The Control Chorus chants a paean of praise in behalf of illegal work, the heroism needed in order to rouse the masses to engage in the class war.

The demonstration proceeds logically, step by step, and each of the moral paradoxes is acted out by the Four Agitators. They gain support among the workers, some of whom go on strike when their wages fall. The Young Comrade is assigned to stand at the gate of the factory and distribute forbidden "literature." He interferes when the policeman on duty strikes a worker, and thus calls attention to himself. The damage is done. Is it right to oppose injustice wherever encountered? The Four Agitators furnish the answer: "He opposed a small injustice. But the great injustice—strike breaking—went right on."[40] The next problem is significantly headed "What Is a Human Being Actually?" The Young Comrade is sent to obtain arms from the merchants, but he muffs his assignment because he cannot keep his tongue under control. Hence the point of the lesson: honor must not be put before higher considerations. When the Young Comrade impatiently demands immediate action, the Agitators tell him:

> Take a look at reality!
> Your revolution is quickly made and lasts one day
> And is strangled the morning after
> But our revolution begins tomorrow
> Conquers and changes the world.[41]

The Young Comrade is obdurate and will not wait; he questions the authority of the party. "Are its thoughts secret, its decisions unknown? Who is the Party?"[42] He holds to his own humane convictions; he will follow the counsel of his heart. He will remove his disguise and appear before the workers in his true identity. He takes off his mask and tears it up, announcing that he and the other agitators have been sent from Moscow. Without his mask, his face is naked, "human, open, guileless."[43] He continues shouting to the workers to rise in revolt. The Agitators are forced to strike him down and flee.

What is to be done? Measures must be taken. The Agitators decide to shoot the Young Comrade and throw him in the lime pit. There is no other way out. It is a terrible thing to do, to kill, but Brecht justifies this necessity:

> But we will kill ourselves and not just others if necessary
> Since only by force can this dying world be changed
> As every living man knows.[44]

The Young Comrade agrees to his own liquidation. He dies as a martyr, repeating the communist credo, affirming the absolute need for revolutionizing the world. The play has shown, as the Control Chorus points out, how much it takes to revolutionize the world.

From *Baal* to *The Measures Taken* represents an extreme swing of the pendulum. The threat of fascism drove Brecht to take a stand. *The Measures Taken* seems to defend the necessary murders. *Mother Courage*, perhaps Brecht's best play, cynically highlights the tragicomic contradictions of a society that is addicted to the suicidal sport of war. *The Caucasian Chalk Circle* is an ideological play which tells a naïvely didactic story within a story. The dramatic framework is provided for the express purpose of preaching the message that the world can be changed. The revolutionary changes which *The Caucasian Chalk Circle* exhibits as having taken place in the past apply directly to the world of today.

Despite the political content of his later plays, Brecht is a highly complex as well as superbly gifted dramatist. Though Brecht never became a dogmatic mouthpiece of the party line, he was in full sympathy with the communist interdiction of romantic individualism in the theater. Rejecting the myth of individualism and the false values this myth embodied, he devoted his talent to the task of disclosing the tragicomedy of appearances. He sought to open the eyes of the workers to the redemptive truth that materialist values are primary. Economics is fate. If he experimented daringly with the technique of alienation, his scope was deliberately restricted to the social theme. He reduced the problematical character of reality to one issue only, that of the class war.

The dominant metaphor in Brecht's plays is that of society. What he stresses is not the individual but the collective ideal. That is why he tried to eliminate as far as possible the subjective element and portray the world as it "really" is. He always interprets reality as social reality; his art, as one critic points out, is "a critical reproduction of reality."[45] That is, in substance, the aesthetic theory propounded by Chernyshevski. Art, Brecht believed, can transform reality by first changing the minds of men. The ultimate aim of "estrangement" in the theater is to overcome the pernicious effect of human alienation, and for that the triumph of communism is necessary. Since communism is, theoretically, supposed to be based on scientific premises, Brecht endeavored to create epic dramas that would be in conformity with the scientific outlook.

In such a dramatic universe, the individual is demoted to a position of relative insignificance; the emphasis is not on his uniqueness but on what he has in common with his class. Brecht, however, was too good a dramatist to make his work conform mechanically to Marxist principles or the formal prescriptions of socialist realism. Though he never faltered in his efforts to make social reality rather than theatrical illusion prevail, he relied on irony, polarity, and ambiguity to preserve the structural complexity of his plays so that vision frequently overrides ideology. His epic theater was non-Aristotelian only in the sense that it was Marxist in its orientation. It elevates social reality to the status of an absolute. For Brecht, society is God. Absent from his work are the metaphysical problems that torment the mind of playwrights like Lenormand, Andreyev, Samuel Beckett, and Ionesco. For Ionesco, who intensely dislikes Brecht's dramas, "there is no art without metaphysics, and there is no society away from its nonsocial context."[46] Politicalized drama, he argues, provides but a narrowly delimited view of the world. He looks upon the drama of "commitment" as a catastrophe, and from the metaphysical perspective of the absurd it is that.

5. ENVOI

The social dimension cannot be excluded from the literary domain. Man exists at all times in a social milieu and his life is in many important respects shaped by it, but his life is also inescapably personal and private. He chooses himself in choosing the kind of life he leads; he is responsible for the actions he initiates and even, as Freud tells us, for the dreams he dreams. At the same time, he cannot secede from society. He may declare himself an outlaw, but even in his rebelliousness he does not cut himself off from the parent body of mankind. The dualism between private and public, individual and social, is based on a factitious distinction. The alienated artist of the twentieth century is hostile to society because it fails to live up to his conception of what it should be. In his opposition to industrialism, mechanization, wage slavery, and the almighty power of the cash nexus, he is actuated at bottom by a vision of what is truly human, by a desire to purify and regenerate the life of man. Art is thus more than a means of self-expression; it bridges the gulf that separates man from man. The artist does not create in solitude for himself alone. He writes for other men, but he is not for that reason subservient to the society of his age.

Every character he introduces, however sharply individualized, is a microcosmic representation of his society. Whereas the writer committed to communism delineates how social and historical necessity triumphs over the will of individuals, one can best render the life of society in literature by concentrating attention on the individual hero, who incarnates the value of a whole society. The social perspective, when it is imaginatively rather than dogmatically embodied in literature, does not transform the individual and his personal relationships into examples of the social process in action. As Raymond Williams says: "Every aspect of personal life is radically affected by the quality of the general life, yet the general life is seen at its most important in completely personal terms."[47] The idea of society cannot be abolished by a solipsist fiat; it is always there. No one is isolated. Man lives in society, but in the realm of literature sociological factors are not of paramount importance in the depiction of reality. No two human beings interpret their existential situation in the same way. Man is not simply the fated victim of objective historical necessity. The social perspective, however fundamental, is not the only one or the most essential one that literature can rely upon in its portrayal of the human condition.

From the point of view of method, it is not the distilled thought, the paraphrasable ideas, of a work that count but its artistic insight and imaginative power. Art has today progressively cut itself off from politics, philosophy, and religion. It no longer serves a purpose which the entire community can accept. It does not borrow and perpetuate the ready-made attitudes of the past; it is exploratory, even heretical, in its quest for the truth of reality. The frame of reference has been relativized; the writer is now more or less on his own. Art performs its wonted ritualistic function but no longer under the aegis of the ecumenical church or the party. Though the writer is situated in the present and his language, like his form, is tied to his age, his work says something which transcends his time. Everything, even his utopian visions, depends on the way he views the world and the nature of man.

1. POLITICAL MESSIANISM IN THE NINETEENTH CENTURY

THE CHIEF identifiable traits of political messianism lie in its opposition to religion. The realm of the supernatural must be liquidated so that the way will be prepared for the establishment in the immediate or remote future of the kingdom of heaven on earth. As religion declined toward the end of the eighteenth century, the messianic impulse made itself felt in the sphere of politics.[1] Political messianism is dominated more strongly by the need to achieve social unification than to release the spiritual energies that make for freedom. It assumes that man is capable of building the foundations of the heavenly city on earth with his own hands. If men are wanting in the qualities that insure perfection, it is because of the social chains that bind them.

The utopian mystique is a secular, rationalist perspective. It is characterized almost invariably by limitless faith in human nature and in the power of reason to solve the problems that beset the individual and society. Whereas in the past the men of religious faith were convinced that man was a frail, finite creature of dust and that the true kingdom would be found beyond this world, the utopian believers were determined to impose their will on benighted mankind and erect at once the walls of the city of the sun, for nothing, absolutely nothing, lay on the other side of death. Hence the justification for the exercise of supreme power, the casuistic defense of tyranny, all in the name of realizing a noble ideal. What makes this threat a formidable one in the twentieth century is the triumph of the technological revolution. The political leaders of the world are now in possession of efficient machinery for carrying out their plans, regardless of the cost and the danger involved. "The yearning to take a step toward eternal happiness, toward pure reason and triumphant rationality runs afoul of the danger of global suicide."[2]

While the dream of utopian perfection seized hold of some minds, the artist in the nineteenth century suffered from the painful malady of alienation. Opposed to bourgeois values, the cult of conformity, the worship of Mammon, he gloried in his role of rebel, though he was not at all happy in his isolation. He felt guilty for devoting himself solely to creative pursuits instead of following a "constructive" life of action; he craved, like Zarathustra, to leave his mountain retreat and descend to the valley where he would preach his gospel of redemption to the multitude whom at heart he despised. He yearned to test the truth of his vision by plunging into the heart of reality, by organizing or joining some communal group.[3] Coleridge ardently dreamed of Pantisocracy, the utopian commonwealth to be established on the banks of the Susquehanna. Southey, upon reading William Godwin's *Enquiry concerning Political Justice*, published in 1793, became an enthusiastic convert.[4]

A widely read book (which profoundly influenced young Shelley), Godwin's *Political Justice* preached a doctrine of rationalism carried to the highest degree. A philosophical anarchist, Godwin followed the empiricism of Condillac and conceived of the mind as a bundle of sensations. Character, he held, is shaped decisively by the environment. External circumstances make us what we are. All men, he argued, are potentially capable of living according to the dictates of pure reason. All that is needed to transform the character of men is to get them to perceive the true nature of things. Godwin hoped that his principles, if consistently acted on, would bring about a utopian social order. Shelley's *Queen Mab* preached the gospel of science and humanitarianism.

The last two cantos presented his conception of the Golden Age, the vision of perfectibility at last attained. There is no serpent of evil in this Shelleyan paradise. Man acts freely out of his own goodness of heart.

It is in *Prometheus Unbound* that Shelley reverses the meaning of the myth of Prometheus. Instead of showing that the punishment meted out to the rebel was deserved, the hero hurls his oppressor down to everlasting oblivion. Shelley rejected the idea that Prometheus sinned. Submission to necessity, to which Zeus himself is subject—that is the essence of evil. Man must not submit, but he can triumph only by eradicating the evil in his own heart, his fear and hate, his resentment against the nature of things. In this way, though still conforming to the laws of nature, he would no longer be their slave. Shelley thus turns Prometheus into a moral hero, a savior, while Zeus is made to personify the force of evil. Not that the universe is evil. No, Zeus represents the evil in the mind of Prometheus and of mankind in general. The downfall of Zeus symbolizes the overthrow of the established order. *Prometheus Unbound* goes beyond Godwin's social philosophy in that it embodies Shelley's belief that man is enslaved by the evil in his own being and that this evil can be overcome by the power of love.

In the nineteenth as in the twentieth century, what motivates the imaginative construction of utopian fantasies is the desire for unflawed happiness on earth. The vision of modern utopia, which grows out of faith in science, represents the Promethean will of man in his efforts to impose control over nature. Man chooses the purpose he will live by. His destiny now rests securely in his own hands. This is the secular "religion" which animates the humanistic writers of utopias in modern times. But when this dream, like the dream of reason deified in the French Revolution, was put to the test, it resulted in widespread disillusionment. A number of dissident voices were raised.

Brook Farm had gained the eager support of a group of young intellectuals, but it enlisted one member who was no believer in the then regnant gospel of social reform. Though Nathaniel Hawthorne felt no genuine affinity with Brook Farm or the ideals to which it was dedicated, he decided to join the community in 1841. He wished to devote himself to writing rather than farming, but he lacked the privacy he found necessary for his creative work, and so it was not long before he decided to leave. What was he, a writer of romances, doing cutting hay or hauling manure? He had other more important talents to put to use.

Hawthorne, in *The Blithesdale Romance*, which is a "romance" and not a realistic or documentary portrayal of life at Brook Farm, is prophetic in his rejection of utopian humanism. He does not share the hope that man, scientifically enlightened, would carry forward the process of evolutionary development to undreamed-of heights. That is the hubristic faith which has animated a number of writers in the twentieth century. H. G. Wells emphasized the radical difference that separated the utopian writers of his time from those who came before Darwin; now man is in a position to take command of the forces that make for optimum growth. Utopia ceases to be a condition of static perfection; it is part of a process of evolution that never stops.

2. H. G. WELLS AND THE MODERN SCIENTIFIC UTOPIA

The object of this chapter is not to draw up a detailed survey of literary utopian schemes in the last two centuries. My object is to analyze the view of the world and of man that the utopian perspective presupposes. The Promethean myth, as it finds expression in H. G. Wells's *A Modern Utopia* (1905), boldly proclaims faith in the possibilities of endless progress. The characters in utopian fantasies of this type are humanity writ large; they embody the ideal of perfection to be realized on earth. Man becomes like a god. Abandoning the absurd notion of personal immortality, he knows that he lives on in mankind. Each one is privileged to participate in an epic march of humanity, onward and upward. As for what happens when perfection is finally attained, the utopian writers stoutly reaffirm their optimism, but they cannot entirely banish the anguish of metaphysical doubt. The ontological mystery still remains, even though the new Adam is now able to trace the overall design of the cosmic process. Will science be enough to sustain man, especially when it makes clear that some day all life on earth will perish in glacial death? Man conquers matter and space, but he cannot escape the fate of ultimate extinction. The evolutionary fantasy of the modern Prometheus is haunted by the nightmarish fear that man may be superseded by other forms of life—perhaps by a race of ants. That is the frightening vision Wells describes in *The War of the Worlds* (1898).

What Wells is saying in *The War of the Worlds* is that civilization with all its scientific expertise and productive capability may be doomed to go under. And *The Time Machine*, though formally a piece of utopian fiction, is actually one of the first modern antiutopian fantasies, showing to what the class conflict might lead in the remote future: a world inhabited not by perfect men but by an enfeebled race which lives in dreadful fear of the Morlocks, the workers underground who feed cannibalistically on their bodies. The epilogue tells us that the Time Traveler "thought but cheerlessly of the advancement of mankind, and saw in the growing pile of civilization only a foolish heaping that must inevitably fall back upon and destroy its makers in the end."[5]

Evolution and technology provide the basis of utopian hope, but these developments, especially technological specialization, call forth a profoundly pessimistic reaction. The dangers of mechanization are not to be minimized. The machine is a monster that may run amok. Indeed, the early scientific fantasies of Wells reveal no utopian optimist; they give expression to "a kind of fatalistic pessimism, combined with intellectual scepticism."[6] In "The Extinction of Man," an essay published originally in 1894, Wells speculates that the end of the race of man might be brought about by a new kind of predatory ant or an enlarged breed of land-crab.[7]

Early in the twentieth century, Wells gradually abandoned his pessimistic outlook and began to draw a more romantic picture of human possibilities. He turned away steadily from literature as art to literature as sociology and preachment. His *A Modern Utopia* has been called the first modern utopia, but it was also, with the exception of *Walden Two*, the last modern utopia.[8] The faith he cherished in illimitable human progress has been shattered. The utopian expectations of this militant liberal, his demand for the maximum use of intelligence and the scientific coordination of human energy in solving the problems of the world, all this has been largely discredited. His scientism, his belief in the infallible virtues of social engineering, were based on "a radically immature view of human existence."[9]

The trouble with the utopian is that he is presumptuous in his ambitions for mankind. He means well, to be sure; he hopes to promote the common welfare and contribute to the happiness of humanity at large, but the method he proposes to use to effect his ends gives rise to fierce controversy and inevitable opposition. Wells might declare that he retained his skepticism, but on one issue at least he entertained no doubt: namely, the desirability of founding the utopian commonwealth. Like Chernyshevski, he is supported in his "faith" by his reliance on the scientific method. His basic assumption is that the nature of man can be improved.

Wells is aware that the chief difficulty confronting the utopian engineers is the problem of preserving the freedom of the individual while endeavoring at the same time to achieve the highest degree of communal integration. The members must somehow be made to desire what is best for the group as a whole. If the ideal state is to be established, however, it must be done by a drastic process of unification. Collectivization entails the loss of individual freedom, while uncurbed individualism leads to the danger of oppression by the few. Wells is confident that these problems can be solved by the use of scientific controls. He looks forward eagerly to a future in which mechanical energy will replace the need for physical labor. In fact, he predicts that there appears "no limit to the vision of life by the machine."[10] It is this faith in the machine which is the essential feature of modern utopia. If the specialists in the various fields would pool their knowledge in the form of a world encyclopedia, this would furnish the basis for the answers to *all* the questions the mind of man might raise. Wells confesses that he likes his world "coherent and consistent."[11] But if the world is to be made coherent and consistent, then the differences which divide human beings do not constitute an insuperable obstacle.[12]

Wells, in short, is the exemplary liberal who believes in the supreme power of reason. Like his hero in *A Modern Utopia*, he feels in order to think. Like his hero, too, he desires to live in a tidy universe, to construct a world that is rational in all its parts. He was confident for a time that his dream would come true. The whole world would be shaping "the fair and great and fruitful World State, that will only not be Utopia because it will be this world."[13] Unfortunately, the excesses of the utopian imagination culminated in a mood of bitter disenchantment. In *Mind at the End of Its Tether* (1945), Wells bade farewell to his dream of utopian idealism. Freedom turned out to be not only a burden but a curse. If science endowed man with amazing power over his environment, it also led him to invent—and then use—the atom bomb. Paradoxically enough, the theory of relativity and developments in the field of nuclear physics forced him to face the truth of his own insignificance in the scheme of things. The curious upshot of all this utopian indulgence is that after the First

World War and increasingly thereafter a vigorous antiutopian movement sprang up.

3. *ANTIUTOPIANISM IN MODERN LITERATURE*

Futurism and Archaism are, both alike, attempts to break with an irksome Present by taking a flying leap out of it into another reach of the stream of Time without abandoning the plane of mundane life on Earth. And these two alternative ways of attempting to escape from the Present but not from the Time-dimension also resemble one another in the further point of being *tours de force* which prove, on trial, to have been forlorn hopes. The two movements differ merely in the direction—up or down the Time-stream—in which they make their two equally desperate sorties from a position of present discomfort and distress which neither the futurist nor the archaist has any longer the heart to hold.[14]

Few historians have written on the problem of futurism with as much wide-ranging scholarship and psychological insight as Toynbee, and few, in their study of the lessons of the past, have been as fertile and suggestive in making pointed comparisons with the contemporary situation.[15] For futurism, the ground preempted by the utopian mentality, runs counter to the grain of human nature; though men are tempted to flee from an unpleasant present into a more consoling past, they would rather cling to the present, no matter how disagreeable it may be, than plunge into a frightening unknown future. But the most appalling feature of utopian futurism is that it is intrinsically "totalitarian" in its plan of conquest; it breaks violently and completely with the past. Fortunately, futurism, like archaism, has its limits; the goal it pursues so strenuously cannot be attained, though this does not mean that the goal is necessarily without value. The important lesson Toynbee has to teach the present "lost generation" (every generation in the twentieth century is "lost" in its own way) is that futurism, despite its scientifically nurtured optimism, is essentially motivated by despair. When the past can no longer save us, the utopian mind turns desperately toward the future in the hope that it can recoup its losses and realize its bankrupt dreams.

Not that ideals of social perfection are to be scorned as quixotic. Ideals, no matter how impracticable, do present an ambitious and often attractive program of reform, and we must not criticize such schemes by applying the pragmatic yardstick of immediate possibilities.[16] Is it not true that men strive to realize the full force of their ideal even against the stubborn, irreducible opposition of things? Once an idea enters human consciousness, it is difficult to drive out. It grows and multiplies and gathers increasing strength and momentum. Interpreting reality in the light of the utopian perspective, the scientific futurist gradually forms the conviction that it is the truth and the way.

In literature, certainly, the romantic impulse would peter out were it not for the vital, fructifying influence of the utopian dream. Without the compelling vision of a more perfect world before him, the futurist writer would lose much of his creative élan. As we have seen, Shelley, the archromanticist, the lyrical evangelist of that golden age to be inaugurated in the future, believed if each man expelled the evil from his heart, the movement toward social perfection would be irresistible. Shelley believed this—believed it with all his heart. Here is a beautiful spirit, pardlike, tameless, intoxicated with a vision of the infinite perfectibility that man, the master of his own destiny, might attain:

> Equal, unclassed, tribeless and nationless,
> Exempt from awe, worship, degree, the king
> Over himself.

Shelley's vision is still with us today, voiced with equal, if not greater, evangelical fervor. Promethean man will not be deterred from spying out the secrets of nature and exploring the outermost limits of space. Science manifestly works; it is only a failure of nerve that prompts some men to draw back from the consequences wrought by the scientific revolution. The technological prophets of our time are confident that posthistoric man, by his application of technology on a global scale, will transform all aspects of life and bring on the advent of the millennium. They impatiently sweep aside what they describe as "the mene-tekel utopias,"[17] which are meant to show what antihuman horrors are brought into being by this mania for scientifically managed perfection. Antiutopian writers issue "senseless warnings against the inevitable, instead of trying to understand it."[18] Man can rise above his finite limitations. He is no longer the measure. Hence a new aesthetic is imperatively called for that will get rid of the burdensome and obsolete traditions of the preceding century. A new world, a world transfigured, is coming to birth. Relativity is now being brought within the realm of sensory experience. The exploration of space, once it has been accomplished, will steadily change the mind of man as he begins to integrate his awareness of the fourth dimension and makes it a functional part of his outlook.

Despite these dogmatic pronouncements based on the theory of relativity, contemporary civilization has gone far in its repudiation of utopian fantasies; the very word "utopian" is in bad repute, even among the Marxist intellectuals. The term is full of hidden ambiguities. The epithet "Utopian" became a potent weapon in the campaign the communists waged against non-Marxist socialism. On one side was scientific engineering and objective truth and on the other sentimentality and delusion. As Martin Buber declares: "To be a 'Utopian' in our age means: to be out of step with modern economic development, and what modern development is we learn of course from Marxism."[19] Buber is firmly of the belief that society cannot be regenerated until we are prepared to tap the full *spiritual* resources of mankind. Since the goal is perfection, it is dangerous for the utopian ideal to be converted into a socioeconomic and technological system. More is at stake than replacing one social order with another, and what is at stake, as Buber maintains, "is nothing less than man's whole existence."[20] In the collective state, whether of the right or the left, the human being loses his personal identity, "ceases to be the living member of a social body and becomes a cog in the 'collective' machine."[21]

Marxism itself, far from being a science of society, as its followers like to think, is shot through with utopian, messianic elements. Trotsky, in picturing the socialist paradise to be established in the future, hails the miracles that will be performed by the machine. Technology constitutes a new "faith" that can actually cut down mountains and move them. "Through the machine, man in Socialist society will command nature in its entirety."[22] Communist life will be intelligently planned and efficiently organized so that man will no longer be under the capricious rule of nature. Then Trotsky pens the following apocalyptic passage, which is the communist version of *Prometheus Unbound*. It goes beyond Shelley's ecstatic vision in its prediction that man will be able, through the achievements of science and technology, to conquer the fear of death.

The human race will not have ceased to crawl on all fours before God, kings and capital, in order later to submit humbly before the dark laws of heredity and a blind sexual selection! Emancipated man will want to attain a greater equilibrium in the work of his organs and a more proportional developing and wearing out of his tissues in order to reduce the fear of death to a rational reaction of the organism toward danger.[23]

Though some visionary voices of utopian idealism are still to be heard, in the second half of the twentieth century there are few dream-architects who are prepared to draw up a blueprint of the earthly paradise of the future (it is always situated in the future; "Man never is, but always to be, blest"). Faith in scientific potentialities now must be tempered by a sober appraisal of conditions as they actually exist and by a grim knowledge of history as it has been forged in fire and blood during the past fifty years. The market in social utopias has dropped to its lowest point. Many historical factors have contributed to this rising tide of disillusionment. The antiutopian swing is caused, directly or indirectly, by the failure of the Soviet experiment and by the disenchantment brought about by Stalin's brutal dictatorship over the proletariat. As a result, the intellectuals of the West have become noticeably less optimistic in what they expect of the future. History, far from marching toward some grandiose consummation in the fullness of time, may utterly disappoint the hopes of man. The future may give rise to worse nightmares than the past. "Not progress denied but progress realized, is the nightmare haunting the anti-utopian novel."[24] In general, the novel of this type focuses attention sharply on the dangers of the utopian obsession.

The antiutopian impulse made itself felt in England as far back as 1932, just at the time during the depression decade when many of the hopeful intellectuals of the West were embracing the communist doctrine. *Brave New World*, by Aldous Huxley, pictures the robot paradise of the future. Huxley later felt that he could have furnished a third alternative in this work: the possibility of salvation to be gained by the community of exiles and refugees from the Brave New World, who would use technology and science "as though, like the Sabbath, they had been made for man, not . . . as though man were to be adapted and enslaved to them. Religion would be the conscious and intelligent pursuit of man's Final End."[25] It is doubtful if Huxley would have improved much upon the first version of *Brave New World* if he had revised it in the light of his changed mystical perspective.[26] At the time he composed the novel he did not perceive the full implications of his protest. The utopian nightmare he had imagined is more imminent than he had originally suspected. Perhaps it will become true by the end of this century, if by then we do not succeed in destroying ourselves.

In *Ape and Essence*, written sixteen years later, after the atomic bomb had been dropped on Hiroshima, Huxley holds science chiefly responsible for many of the ills that have befallen mankind. *Ape and Essence* visualizes the end of civilization after the Third World War. We see man's glassy essence, playing such fantastic tricks before high heaven as would make the angels weep. Huxley rubs in the apocalyptic horror by dwelling circumstantially on the effects of the disease induced by chemicals and the mass destruction caused by atomic armaments. The scientists now in the employ of various governments—it is they who are the unregenerate baboons, dedicated to the fiendish task of inventing lethal agencies that will finally kill off everybody on earth. The Narrator in *Ape and Essence* describes our age of anxiety, its paroxysms of hate and terror, its agonized efforts to escape the deluge of death. "There is no longer a man among his fellow men . . . there is only a lacerated animal, screaming and struggling in the trap. For in the end fear casts out even a man's humanity. And fear . . . fear is the very basis and foundation of modern life. Fear of the science which takes away with one hand what it so profusely gives with the other."[27] This is the collective madness from which we suffer.[28] The result of trying to conquer Nature is bound to be universal disaster.

If Huxley, disgusted with secular politics, renounced the ways of the world and accepted the will of God, there were others who were shaken out of their utopian fixation without turning to religion. George Orwell first learned the facts of political life, the truth about Stalinism, when he volunteered to fight in the Spanish Civil War on the Loyalist side. *Animal Farm* and *1984* are the fictional records of his progressive disillusionment with Russian communism. *1984* is not meant to be a fantastically improbable fable about the enslavement of man in the future; it is the savagely delineated portrait of a condition that actually obtains today. Now that man has lost faith in himself, he has ceased to believe in the future. The mass-man, the ape-man, anonymous and conditioned in thought and behavior, infests the earth. Objective truth is outlawed as a bourgeois superstition. History is falsified. The state, in full control of all the media of communication, dictates what truth is. Individualism is taboo. There is no privacy. The Party has devised scientific ways of getting inside a person and making him believe anything it wishes.

Equally portentous is the warning Koestler sounds in *The Age of Longing*. A sad, bitterly disenchanted novel, it gives a prophetic forecast of the events that would probably take place in the 1950s. It diagnoses the ideological cancer that is eating away at the vitals of European culture, weakening its will to resist. Europe is disintegrating because it has accepted the finality of personal death. If personal death is final, then God does not exist. Koestler points out how the lost cosmic consciousness has been replaced by the worship of the new Baal: society. As Julien, the most far-sighted of the communist exiles in the novel, expresses it:

I don't mean the worship of the Totalitarian State, or even of the State as such: the real evil is the deification of society itself. Sociology, social science, social therapy, social integration, social what-have-you. Since we have accepted death as final, society has been replacing the cosmos. Man has no longer any direct transactions with the universe, the stars, the meaning of life; all his cosmic transactions are monopolised and all his transcendental impulses absorbed by the fetish "Society."[29]

If society is worshiped as an absolute that supplants the metaphysical and religious vision, it is science that is principally to blame. Science has made man inordinately proud. The scientific utopia is based on the assumption that man is God and the research scientist is his prophet. Man is but a physical organism, part of a complex social structure, both of which can be controlled. The individual, by being absorbed harmoniously in the social whole, thereby manages to achieve a "higher" destiny. If scientific utopias have nevertheless been found wanting, it is because they run counter to the irrepressible human craving for freedom. They leave out of account the finitude of the human being; they represent a Promethean assertion of will which ignores the cosmic dimension and man's mortal fate. The utopian scientist dismisses these objections as metaphysically specious and grandly affirms his faith in humanity. "The reason why people believe that a scientific world order is impossible, or that even if it were possible it would not be worth while, lies in a deep-seated lack of faith in humanity."[30]

And indeed what is there that can possibly be regarded as harmful in the utopian ideal? One recent champion of the cause declares: "We all would prefer a life of brotherhood, equality, joy, leisure, plenty, peace, health, and a life of permanent, unrelieved, universal *satisfaction*: is there anyone who would not?"[31] This is a loaded question he asks. He leaves out the element of the irrational and the unpredictable in man. He sweeps aside as irrelevant the refractory metaphysical factor, the ontological mystery, the awareness of death, the fear and trembling Kierkegaard describes, the anxiety that Kafka evokes, the transcendental impulses Koestler speaks of. These, we are told, should not concern those men who are striving to establish individual and collective life on a rational basis. Hence the utopian engineer is perfectly willing to map out plans which call for the suppression of those individuals who stand in the way of the collective millennium.

That is the saving message broadcast in *Walden Two*, by B. F. Skinner, one of the most militant exponents of the science of human and social engineering. In *Science and Human Behavior*, he assumes that man is a machine. He studies human behavior in terms derived from the world of physics, even if he has to dispose of the problem of human freedom. Science, he is convinced, makes for survival: that is all we know and all we need to know. His utopianism is, not unexpectedly, the expression of a scientific relativism that has been ideologically converted into an absolute.

4. THE SCIENTIFIC UTOPIA

Walden Two describes in expository rather than novelistic form a scientific utopia established somewhere in the United States: one, we are assured, that works. It works because it is based squarely on the science of human engineering and therefore allows for no errors. By conditioning the variable stuff of human nature, it eliminates those sources of error and conflict which were responsible for the failure of previous utopian colonies. In short, what we get is not only an impassioned plea for efficient and harmonious communal living but an equally impassioned argument in favor of a science of human nature. "Behavioral engineering"—this is the key metaphor in this fictional dissertation. It furnishes a leading clue to Skinner's conception of man and his doctrinaire interpretation of reality.

The utopian scientist is as obsessed in his way as the true believer. He is convinced he has found the cure for all the evils that afflict mankind. Frazier, the hero as benevolent scientist, is in love with facts and statistics. He enjoys nothing better than to discourse at length "about his beloved behavioral engineering or of man's triumph over nature."[32] He acknowledges that the problem of organizing an economically self-sufficient community is relatively easy compared to the formidable task of transforming the character of man. Yet even in this psychological realm of character-building Frazier remains confident that the proper manipulation of the environment will produce the desired results. He is all for manipulation, control, experimentation, human engineering, scientific conditioning. As for antisocial emotions, these can be removed from the "behavioral repertoire." "It's simply a matter of behavioral engineering."[33] The secret is out: these scientific utopians are searching for some "method of shaping human behavior by imparting techniques of self-control."[34]

Walden Two offers numerous examples of behavioral engineering in action. The unintentional irony of the novel emerges in Frazier's sincere conviction that the science of human behavior will produce the ideal cooperative state in which perfect freedom flourishes. The goal steadily aimed at is to effect an optimum degree of prediction and control in the social sciences. Hence Frazier, who speaks for the author, has no use for metaphysical speculation as to what makes up the good life. Men *know* what it is without theorizing about it. The good life values health, seeks to reduce the burden of unpleasant labor, and provides opportunities for people to fulfill themselves socially and creatively. As for "happiness," no effort is made to impose that on the group. Frazier exclaims: "We don't *use* force! All we need is adequate behavioral engineering."[35] Technological utopianism is obviously based on a number of antimetaphysical metaphysical premises.

There is no religion in *Walden Two*. Frazier patiently explains that not theology but science furnishes the rationale for the new conception of man. There are no absolutes. The otherworldly hopes of Christianity become irrelevant and absurd when the kingdom of heaven is already in existence on earth.[36] As for the phenomenon of death, that, too, is a simple matter of funereal engineering. The pressing need of the age is to hit upon a scientific solution to the life problem. Change is the ruling principle of life. Though the name of Walden Two was chosen in honor of Thoreau's experiment in living for one, the New England transcendentalist would have been horrified by Frazier's remark: "As the science of behavioral engineering advances, less and less is left to personal judgment."[37]

Walden Two has succeeded in purging its society of myth, of heroes, of the fictions spawned by history. Only the Now is real. "It's the only thing we can deal with, anyway, in a scientific way."[38] Even personal relations under the reign of scientism will be reduced to rational principles. Everything—love, marriage, children, hobbies, art, even death—becomes a matter of behavioral engineering. The individual is naught, the community is all. Everything is planned in advance for the good of society, which means that in practice men must be controlled for their own good. Only those who believed in the reality of human freedom would argue against a society based on the science of behavior. As Frazier sums it up neatly: "If man is free, then a technology of behavior is impossible."[39]

Frazier is unshaken in his view that it is now possible to control human behavior. He denies "that freedom exists at all. I must deny it—or my program would be absurd. You can't have a science about a subject matter which hops capriciously about. Perhaps we can never *prove* that man isn't free; it's an assumption. But the increasing success of a science of behavior makes it more and more plausible."[40] The important thing (it is a tall order) is to get people to do what they really want to do. Power must rule somehow, even in a democracy, if the desirable behavioral patterns are to be established. Democracy, however, is not the best form of government, "because it's based on a scientifically invalid conception of man. It fails to take account of the fact that in the long run *man is determined by the state*."[41] At this point, Frazier comes perilously close to the communist view of the relation of the individual to the state. The individual is expendable. Life is not sacred. The state is immortal.

Apart from its structural deficiencies as fiction, *Walden Two* is weak even as an imaginatively embroidered ideology. It makes little provision for intellectual conflict and a balance of forces. The devil is not permitted to speak. God's advocate, because he is a behaviorist, is always in the right. Only the facts count. The triumph of communal living under scientific control is the crowning achievement of man. Frazier declares: "We must never be free of that feverish urge to push forward which is the saving grace of mankind."[42] But this, despite his contempt for philosophy, is clearly a metaphysical utterance. Why the Faustian urge? Why this craving for progress without end or this rooted faith in the science of man? Frazier's program is "essentially a religious movement freed of any dallying with the supernatural and inspired by a determination to build heaven on earth."[43]

Skinner's work of fiction is didactic in aim and therefore often tedious in content. The earthly paradise he projects contains no dark places; all is radiant light. In this technological Garden of Eden no serpent crawls; the fruit blooms on the tree of knowledge and is plucked and eaten, with no dire aftereffects. No villain spins the plot. Human nature is conditioned into desiring what is "good." This points to the flagrant shortcoming of *Walden Two* both as fiction and as scientific prophecy: all the surprises are left out, the cosmic consciousness is conditioned out of existence, there are no mysteries or complications in life. The intimations of the tragic vision are utterly missing. Since behavior is reduced to a series of routine patterns, moral dilemmas do not arise. The individual gladly surrenders his freedom of will, which is only a foolish illusion.[44] The scientific utopia, by making life perfectly secure, removes from the world the bracing challenge of contingency, the element of the unpredictable and the unknowable, the knowledge that between the idea and the reality there falls the Shadow. As George Kateb points out cogently,

Everything in Utopia works to discourage the idea that life is an existentially serious problem requiring a spiritual response. Death, of course, remains; but the categories of anxiety, despair, and human corruption wither away. The spirit, without evil, withers away. If utopia eliminates sin, it also eliminates grace.[45]

To be antiutopian does not mean that one is churlishly opposed to progress (what is progress?) or the cause of human betterment (how is that to be defined and by whom?), but that one recognizes the insuperable limitations of human nature, especially the fact that life must end in death. It is the tragic sense of life that conflicts with the utopian ideal. The question of social goals and ends cannot be disseverd from the question of the character and ultimate destiny of man. History is short-lived; time is still the enemy. Human life may eventually be wiped out by the action of entropy, if not more immediately by radioactive fallout. But the technological engineers, who are determined to leave nothing to chance, are not troubled by such meaningless metaphysical speculations. For them the idea of society takes the place of the idea of God. The truth is one, and science is the religion of truth.

The theory of relativity, the principle of indeterminacy, is transformed into a totalitarian dogmatism that assures man secular salvation, without sin and without grace. The most grievous failing of utopianism of this kind is that in accepting the scientific perspective as the only valid one, it supports a dismal and distorted conception of the nature of man and a mechanically restricted version of reality.

1. THE MECHANICAL MYTH

THE PROBLEM of reality has always troubled the mind of man. He assumes that the world he lives in, unchanging in essence, is there to be known, or, if mysteriously subject to change, is not completely unintelligible. And yet in the course of time he interprets this world in startlingly different ways. Unlike the man of the Middle Ages, twentieth-century man beholds the universe as a whirlwind of energy that has no concern for human woe. In *The Dynasts*, Hardy voiced his stubborn conviction that the Supreme Mover was unknowing, neither moral nor immoral but amoral and irrational. Viewing the universe from the perspective afforded by science, many a poet today finds it impossible to conceive of nature as the great mother, as a moral teacher, or as the Over-Soul. Modern writers are as a rule fully aware of the *philosophic* implications of science; they cannot ignore the challenge posed by their scientific culture; but most of them definitely do not feel at home in a world of electrons, neutrons, vectors, gravitational fields, and electromagnetic forces.

One must consider the singular paradox that the modern Prometheus has become a wretched "outsider." Never before in the history of civilization has man been in such superb command of his technological instruments. He dwells in a highly mechanized environment, he is an integrated part of a huge and supremely efficient productive apparatus, but precisely because this is so does he feel his alienation so keenly. He has been deprived of his former organic relationship to cosmic reality. His confused or dismayed vision of the universe is conditioned by his very technological mastery; he keeps in step with the industrial rhythm of his age; he obeys the call of the public clock and it becomes his private chronometer as well. He becomes the slave of habit and automatic routine, so much so that he seems to function like a machine. Victim of a scientifically postulated system of universal determinism, he becomes the victim, too, of the sources of mechanical power he has unleashed. The technological wizard is gradually overwhelmed by the unaccountable feeling that all those things which make up his life are necessary and inevitable and yet somehow unreal. In his brilliant analysis of the dependence of the social sciences of our time on the mechanical metaphors borrowed from the physical sciences, Matson declares: "The tragic history of the breaking of the human image parallels the disintegration of the inner sense of identity . . . in the modern world."[1]

Small wonder that modern man begins to regard himself as essentially insignificant in the total structure of the universe. A cog in a machine, he can no longer rely on his own initiative, judgment, and freedom of will. Things happen to him; he lives vicariously, involved in a vast network of production over which he has no control. He lives by proxy, taking on reality only as the slave of the machine. Ours, for better or worse, as Ernst Jünger maintains, is a technological age in which the worker becomes a faceless tool, his individuality abolished. The worker, says Jünger, "is moved by no restless, Faustian desire, he is distracted by no illusion, his physics are identical with his metaphysics; he is essentially static."[2] What self, as Wylie Sypher pointedly asks, can emerge in a world of atomic fission and collectivistic integration?[3]

The science of physics is scarcely enough to satisfy the spiritual hunger of man. Times of crisis arise when he cannot evade the metaphysical challenge, the question of the ultimate meaning of his terrestrial destiny. The suspicion enters his mind that the triumph of technology may not, after all, be an unmixed blessing. He is not willing to scrap the machinery the ingenuity of the race has perfected; he is frankly grateful for the manifold ways in which applied science has increased its measure of control over the natural environment, but all these developments entail a heavy price. The seemingly "miraculous" powers of science and industry serve to entrench the myth of the machine. Even if industrial society were to achieve optimum results and establish utopian communities all over the habitable earth, science could provide man with no sense of spiritual purpose, no guide for the conduct of his life. Nor could it fulfill Skinner's expectation that by its efficient organization of life on rational principles, it will grant him the ardently desired gift of "happiness."[4] "After all, industrial society is no more than the collection of means to provide the majority of the people with decent material conditions—just that, and not an end."[5]

Obviously man does not believe he *is* a machine nor does he actually behave like one, even when he accepts the Pavlovian or behavioristic interpretation of human nature. He realizes, of course, that computers can be constructed which are capable of solving highly complex problems and of carrying out calculations of the highest magnitude with amazing speed and reliability. According to one computer scientist, Dr. Richard W. Hamming, "A philosophy for the future man-machine combination is yet to be created, but it is time to start searching for one."[6] The undesirable human effects resulting from such a cybernetic revolution must, however, be anticipated. The computers would prove harmful in that they would drastically reduce the area of privacy. The memory of these machines is infallible and ineradicable. Equally damaging, if such technological controls were put into operation, would be the psychological blow delivered to man's self-esteem. For here are complete robots that can react under any specified circumstances—"ingeniously solve problems, compose symphonies, create works of art and literature, and pursue any goals. They can be given any desired behavioral properties."[7] If the Promethean ego of Western man suffered three crippling traumas, the Copernican revolution, the Darwinian theory of the evolution of the species, and the psychoanalytic disclosure of the primacy of the unconscious, the fourth trauma will most likely be administered by advancing technology as the machine progressively outstrips and dominates its creator.

The protest against mechanization came long before Dostoevski's underground man rebelled against the supremacy of reason and mathematics. The eighteenth century believed that the world was perfectly reasonable in structure. God was a magnificent architect who had brought all things together in universal harmony according to the principle of rationality. Cartesian thought thus culminated in a mechanical explanation of the universe, which entailed a systematic depreciation of feeling and imagination as ways of getting to "know" the cosmic order. The contradictions inherent in this philosophy of reason with its mathematical projection of a mathematical God led inevitably to a reaction: a compensatory emphasis upon the life of instinct and imagination. The romantic revolt had, in addition, to cope with the challenge posed by the industrial revolution: the invention of the steam engine, the rapid progress of scientific inquiry, the building of steel bridges, the mushroom growth of factories. William Blake fiercely denounced the mechanical interpretation of the universe that the writings of Bacon, Newton, and Locke tended to support. The protest of the romantic poets in the nineteenth century proved altogether ineffectual. The philosophy of science made steady headway.[8]

As we reach the twentieth century, the conflict between the mechanistic and the spiritual view of reality grows more intense. Scientism seeks to interpret *everything*, including the mind, in terms of mechanical causation. All that we shall ever know of the working of the mind, according to Joseph Needham, "will be mechanistic, expressed in the language of determinism, and related as closely as possible to physico-chemical facts obtained from observation on cerebral metabolism."[9] That would seem to settle the issue once and for all. Science must rely on observation and measurement or it is nothing. It must therefore dispense with metaphysical notions and postulate a mechanistic universe. Though nothing is more painfully disconcerting to the pride of man than this realization that he is but a microscopic speck of energy in the cosmic machine, he must, so the scientific gospel reads, learn to live with it, for it is nothing less than the truth. Needham pens this curious and revealing confession of his faith as a scientist:

Worse still, when he examined himself he could find no reason for thinking what he found there any exception to the laws of motion and of thermo-dynamics, and the usages of the mechanical universe. MAN A MACHINE might be terrible, but it was true . . . . The world which had brought him forth would presently swallow him up: he was a colony and vassal of it. Minute and feeble, powerless to alter one of its dealings with himself, he could gain no satisfaction from it save by cherishing it and studying it in the manner of the scientist.[10]

Whereas Needham confronts the universe with the courageous assertion of his scientific will to truth, Pascal, the mathematician and mystic, is frightened by the eternal silence of the empty spaces.

The machine is without question the most expressive metaphor of our scientific culture. A linguistic usage, a way of speaking, a trick of analogy has been converted into what is now believed by many to be an observable "fact" of nature. Man *is* a machine! The semantic difference between using a metaphor and interpreting it literally is disregarded.[11] Taken literally, the metaphor does violence to what is observed and smuggles in contraband metaphysical entities; it then becomes a myth. The current myth derives from the metaphysics of mechanism. The metaphor which asserts that the world is a machine or man is an animal constitutes a metaphysical perspective, an angle of vision, a device whereby something is pictured in terms of something else. Trouble arises, as is often the case today, when the metaphor is mistaken for the literal truth and the myth identified with reality. Mechanism is but one human way of interpreting the universe. The world is not a machine wound up nor is it blind will personified. The metaphysical veils covering the mechanical metaphor must be torn aside. Oddly enough, it was the scientists themselves who were responsible for unmasking this myth.

The theory of relativity resulted in a radically revised picture of reality. The influence of the observer, his position in the time-space continuum, had to be taken into account. Nature was no longer a uniform field of energy in motion. Uncertainty entered as a disturbing methodological factor into the conceptual framework of cosmology. Probability, not certainty, was within reach of science. The universe ceased to be regarded as a gigantic machine. The observer entered intimately into the process of observation. The element of chance, of indeterminateness, had to be reckoned with. Radical ambiguity makes itself felt in the scientific universe of discourse. Reality is now acknowledged to be, what it has always been, a mystery. As A. S. Eddington remarks: "I very much doubt if any one of us has the faintest idea of what is meant by the reality or existence of anything but our own Egos."[12]

2. *THE LITERARY PROTEST AGAINST MECHANIZATION*

The protest against the mechanization, and therefore dehumanization, of man was not confined to one country. With the exception of Soviet Russia, it was international in scope. The revolt went further than a rejection of the scientific method that supported the technological revolution. Expressionist drama rebelled against the entire system of industrialization that transformed men into automatons. Georg Kaiser, in *Gas* (1917-19), cried out against the forces in the modern world which were turning men into soulless slaves of the machine. In this play the protagonist, the Billionaire's Son, is powerless in his efforts to liberate the workers from their wage slavery. They cannot grasp his meaning when he bids them have the courage to be themselves: "You are men—you represent Humanity . . . . Deliver yourselves from confusion—heal yourselves!—you that have been wounded —be human, human, human!"[13] When the government, which needs gas in its preparation for war, takes over the task of rebuilding the works that had been blown up, the Billionaire's Son asks in despair: "Tell me, where can I find Man? When will he make his appearance—when will he announce his name—Man? When will he understand himself?"[14] The true nature of man cannot be defeated. He will emerge tomorrow, women will give him birth; but in the second part of *Gas* (1920) even that hope is shattered.

Much of the fiction and drama of the twentieth century is taken up with portraying the deadening and dehumanizing effect of mechanization. The "hero" of modern industrialized society is deprived of identity; he becomes a social security number, an anonymous stereotype, a statistic, a mass man, a robot. He is reduced, as Marx had predicted, to a hand, a function, a tool. The machine issues commands and the worker perforce obeys. The will of the individual does not count. Economics and technology are the directors of history. Whereas the Soviet Union exalted the importance of industrial production to a point where the machine became a veritable god,[15] many Western writers attacked the Satanic mills which robbed the workers of their individuality.

Karel Capek was among the first to voice his opposition to the spread of the technological psychosis, whose apocalyptic symbol today is the atomic bomb. In a series of fictional as well as dramatic fantasies, he embodied his belief that human life is not, and should not be, governed by logical categories or by the standards of industrialized efficiency. The myth of the machine is essentially hostile to the poetic and the religious vision. By making man the slave of matter, it strips him of the saving grace—or indispensable illusion—of freedom. That is why Capek, like D. H. Lawrence, turned against the mechanistic mania. Each perspective, the magical, the utopian, the religious, the scientific, the technological, is meant to gratify the needs of man, but no one perspective will serve to gratify all of them. Serious danger arises when one orientation is allowed to get out of hand.

Karel Capek early experimented with the technique of literary perspectivism, which William E. Harkins has defined as "the construction of a cumulative series of viewpoints, each of which contributes something to the entire picture. Perspectivism goes beyond relativism; perspectivism is a cooperative union of various viewpoints to create truth; relativism is simply the skeptical assertion that various viewpoints are possible."[16] As a creative perspectivist Capek included relativism and skepticism in his vision of the world of man. He could find no answer to the questions he raised but he continued to propound the riddles traditionally asked by the Sphinx. The eternal seeker, he was fearful of falling into the trap set by an absolute relativism, for that would constitute a contradiction in terms. He sought to work his way out of the trap by assuming that almost everything is relative. He abandoned his faith in the absolute of truth because it bred the dangerous vice of fanticism. While not giving up his quest for the truth, he would look upon skepticism as fundamentally more valuable than any truth. Man, the finite creature, will have to relinquish his nostalgia for the absolute, and resign himself to life as it is.

Hence Capek repudiated the ideal of the superman. This striving toward the goal of godlike perfection, what was it but a destructive illusion? Progress has its inexorable limits. Capek exposed the harmful consequences that follow from the monstrous obsession of the modern state with quantity, organizational efficiency, and the mechanics of management. *R.U.R.* (1921) is a dramatic satire that depicts the outcome of the struggle between man and the machine. Redemption from toil is a curse instead of a blessing. The reality of human life demands striving, effort, the boon of physical labor. Old Rossum invented the machine-man as a means of demonstrating that God did not exist. The mechanical man represents the spirit of rationalism carried to a logical, and therefore maniacal, extreme. The robot is the creation of scientific genius. If the robots hate mankind and rise up against them, it is because they are cruelly exploited for commercial profit while man, the master, remains idle. In the end the masters are themselves victimized by their instruments. The utopian dream of the technological society turns into a destructive nightmare. As Capek said of his play: "The conception of the human brain has at last escaped from the control of human hands. That is the comedy of science."[17]

Like Samuel Butler before him in *Erewhon*, Capek is warning the world of the catastrophic danger it runs if it proceeds to mechanize the whole of life. Here is a race of admirably functioning robots, without sensations of pain or fear, who would seem to be the ideal helots of humanity. Unfortunately these mechanical creatures refuse to play their prescribed role and revolt against their masters. They cannot be endowed with a rudimentary intelligence, enough to get them to respond beyond the simple level of conditioned reflexes, without also cultivating in time a desire for freedom and an irrational hatred of their oppressor. In their fury of revenge they engage in wholesale massacres until the human species is about to become extinct; there is no known way now of reproducing robots; the formula has been destroyed. Then the miracle takes place: the light of love dawns in the hearts of two robots who, when they couple like animals, will rediscover the secret of generation. Life on earth will renew itself, though Capek offers no hint as to the degree of happiness the robot world of the future will achieve. Capek, in this satire, is saying that the spiritual principle cannot be excluded without maiming the human personality. Capek is not only antiutopian in his outlook; he is opposed to the pernicious tendency to harbor romantic illusions. It is better to accept the world as it is, with all its faults, and in all humility make the best of the human condition.

Though the writers of our time are no social diagnosticians, they portray clearly enough the debasement of the industrial masses. Like Kaiser and Capek, Eugene O'Neill deals with the theme of the mechanization of man. In *The Hairy Ape*, he presents characters whose work has brutalized them and who dwell homeless in a world of dynamos, speed, steel, and electricity. The imagination of a D. H. Lawrence is haunted by his vision of the kind of life workers must lead in a factory-ridden world. If there are masses and classes, he declares, it is the machine that has invented them both. Enslavement to the machine, he warns, breeds neither greatness nor the spirit of love but a grinding, nihilistic hate. He unmasks the myth that technology makes for the good life. On the contrary, it transforms the workers into living corpses who toil for wages.

Though some American novelists have drawn admiring portraits of the captain of industry, the engineer, European writers do not as a rule exalt the technician as hero. They know that the triumph of technology is accompanied by a movement to dispense with metaphysics and mysticism. Opposed to the human world and the dialogue of spirit that makes true communion possible, it has no use for the foolish sentiment of love. Max Frisch, in *Homo Faber*, draws a critical picture of the technologist as hero. Homo Faber had, on principle, distrusted any display of emotion. He had confidently assumed that man was master of his destiny, that everything has a cause which can be ascertained. He had taken it for granted that technological control over nature was man's unique distinction. Only at the end, as he waits for death, does he come to see that in acting on this scientific faith he has denied his own self and wasted his life.

The issue Frisch faces in *The Chinese Wall* is whether there will be a future for mankind. Now that the atomic bomb is in the hands of a number of nations, the world stands at the crossroads. Will some power-hungry leader doom the world to annihilation? Will this be the cataclysmic culmination of Western man's worship of the Moloch of the machine? Frisch's morality play reveals that the individual is as helpless in our nuclear age as in times past. He introduces a gallery of archetypal figures—Napoleon, Pontius Pilate, Brutus, and Columbus, among others—in order to "distance" the contemporary crisis without in any way playing down the tragic import of his theme. Like Brecht, he is not interested in building up a theatrical illusion of realism. He effectively uses the Chinese wall (we have our own walls) as a symbol of the anomalies of history, but the point of view he presents throughout is that of the Contemporary, who is Everyman, at least every intellectual possessed of a conscience.

When Romeo and Juliet appear on the stage, the former immediately announces the central theme:

> "Entropy" and "atom": what are these?
> Somebody speaks, but no one understands.
> "Death by radiation"—what is this?[18]

While they strain to live out their ecstasy, however brief the time that remains to them, Romeo voices the motif of dreadful foreboding. A fearful change has come over life: "The world's become a single grave."[19] If that is to be the outcome of the next war, then

whoever sits on a throne today holds the human race in his hand, their whole history, starting with Moses or Buddha, including the Acropolis, the Temple of Maia, Gothic cathedrals, including all of Western philosophy, Spanish and French painting, German music, Shakespeare and this youthful pair: Romeo and Juliet. And include in it all, our children and our children's children. A slight whim on the part of the man on the throne, a nervous breakdown, a touch of neurosis, a flame struck by his madness, a moment of impatience on account of indigestion—and the jig is up! Everything! A cloud of yellow or brown ashes building up toward the heavens in the shape of a mushroom, a dirty cauliflower—and the rest is silence—radioactive silence.[20]

In twenty-four scenes, *The Chinese Wall* spells out the threat of extinction. The Contemporary enlightens the audience about the revolutionary discovery that energy equals mass times the speed of light squared and that everything else man knows is relative. Time, too, is relative, for it is a function of space. The Contemporary adds: "And there is actually neither time nor space! Nor truth, for we are so created that we can exist only in time and space."[21] Asked if he believes in God, the Contemporary does not know what to say except to repeat the formula that energy equals mass times the speed of light squared, "which means: mass is energy, an ungodly ball of energy. And woe to the world if it goes wrong! And it *does* go wrong."[22]

Man established the law of cause and effect in the place of God and felt he had solved the secret of creation, but suddenly he beheld

an atom with suicidal free will: the radium atom. And then the behavior of the electrons! And matter, the only thing we can count on, what is it? A dance of numbers, a ghostly diagram. So today we have got this far: God, who could not be found in the microscope, still calls us menacingly to the inevitable reckoning. Anyone who does not think of Him has ceased to think.[23]

There is, alas, nothing the intellectual can do to stave off global disaster. He cannot forestall the verdict of destiny simply because he foresees it. "Great and learned persons arise and call to mankind: 'The cobalt bomb, which you are now producing will be the end of you!'—and people go on making the cobalt bomb."[24] For the first time in history, the Contemporary warns, we are faced with the choice whether we wish the human race to survive or perish. If it is to survive, then war must be rendered impossible. Otherwise this earth will become a dead planet on which no lights gleam since there will be no human eyes to catch them.

And empty and blind as his world is God, blind and empty and without creatures of His making: without the mirror of a dying human eye, without our human consciousness of time . . . Asia, Europe, America—meaningless! senseless! lifeless! spiritless! empty of man! empty of God![25]

What Frisch is saying in this parable is that relativism is no longer tenable in an age of atomic fission. Man cannot stand by silent and unconcerned when the choice is one between survival or destruction of the species. Although Frisch provides no solution, he makes it abundantly clear that if the cult of the machine is not halted it can only lead to world catastrophe. What writers like Kaiser, Capek, D. H. Lawrence, and Frisch have done in challenging the primacy of technological values is to defend the right of the self to exist. How man lives is governed fundamentally by his interpretation of reality and by his conception of what he is. Man cannot legitimately be defined in mechanical terms. Physics and chemistry are capable of accounting for the behavior of automatons, but not that of living men who think, feel, doubt, strive, suffer, and feel a sense of responsibility for the decisions they make and the actions they commit.

Science does not encompass the whole of reality. Physicists who are philosophically trained would be the first to admit that their science does not cover all of experience. The philosophy of science can be invoked to yield surprisingly different conclusions. It can be interpreted to read that men are free to choose their own values: free to regard themselves as machines or free to control and put to humane uses the nuclear energy they have discovered. The world is composed not only of sources of physical energy but also of thought, feeling, the craving for beauty, the activity of art, the conflict between good and evil. Human beings are not to be regarded as God's puppets, determined in every thought and action. In his reliance on the machine-image, the determinist pictures God as the creator of a cosmic machine. *Homo faber* makes God in his own image. Whereas writers of the 1920s protested against a determinism that converted men into mere cogs in a universal mechanism, they now see the atomic bomb, the supreme achievement of the mobilized genius of the scientists of the West, as "the greatest of all menaces to the future of mankind."[26]

1. THE UNIVERSE OF SCIENCE

IF THERE IS, as I have contended, a close correlation between the way in which a person (a character on the stage of life or literature) conceives of himself and the way in which he interprets reality, then it follows that psychology and cosmology are closely interrelated. I have already examined the specter that haunts our age: the dread that the machine, of which the atomic bomb is the ultimate expression, will turn the living into the dead. Many so-called normal people are today filled with the fear of nonbeing, the fear "of the possibility of turning, or being turned, from a live person into a dead thing, into a stone, into a robot, an automaton, without personal autonomy of action, an *it* without subjectivity."[1] Here then is psychological science at last confirming the intuitive perceptions of writers like Kafka and Lawrence, who cried out against the forces of depersonalization that technology set in motion. Frequently the protagonist in existentialist literature is troubled by the suspicion that he is *de trop*, that his relationship to things or other human beings is part of a dream-sequence. At other times he berates himself for these foolish introspective fancies and reassures himself that, however much the imagination may lead him astray, the earth exists; the moon and the sun and the stars are real and will remain aeons after he is but a particle of dust.

But how does science picture the world? The scientific method represents, as Nietzsche knew and Vaihinger reaffirmed, but one perspective among many. What is more, the role of the observer, as modern physicists are forced to acknowledge, cannot be left out. The traditional notion of causation has to be dropped. Any attempt to view the world through other than a human perspective is bound to fail. The difference between subjective and objective in the field of science is simply one of degree. Then, too, to search resolutely after the truth, to assume that the truth can be found, and to leave no stone unturned until it has been flushed out of its hiding place—that constitutes, in effect, a "moral" value. And "the truth" which science seeks to elicit is not at all simple. A rose is not a rose is not a rose. The law of identity is an illusion. Matter, when the physicist attempts to comprehend it, turns into pure energy. As Einstein's theory of relativity made clear, there is no absolute object. This is the paradoxical fact which we must grasp if we are to understand not only the age we live in but the literature which characterizes that age.[2] The further science explores the ultimate constituents of the universe the closer it comes to the frontiers of mystery.

There can be no question that science has had an enormous influence on the modern writer's interpretation of the world. Escape this influence he cannot. It makes a great difference if he knows that he lives in an Einsteinian rather than Newtonian universe. There is scarcely a poet, novelist, or dramatist in the twentieth century who has not, for good or evil, been affected by the existing body of scientific knowledge. Quantum mechanics, nuclear physics, determinism, biology, anthropology, Freudianism, logical positivism—these have in various ways shaped the literary mind and its interpretation of reality, and this despite the fact that the two disciplines, the literary and the scientific, cannot be reconciled. Though there is a fruitful process of cross-fertilization between the two cultures, essentially they have different aims and pursue different methods.

Science concerns itself with the observed data that can be subsumed under general laws. It provides what is usually called "public knowledge." Literature, on the other hand, deals with the realm of the private and the personal, with feelings that are "untranslatable," if not ineffable. It works not with the abstract but with the sensuous and the particular, by means of which it shadows forth the universal. It tries to capture the living concreteness of things. Science endeavors to construct a monistic system, whereas literature renders the uniqueness and the diversity of events. The imaginative writer organizes his material so that the multifariousness and complexity of experience takes on unity and meaning. He unites the personal and the social, the concrete and the abstract, inner and outer, microcosm and macrocosm. Though he has been conditioned by the scientific currents of his age, the scientific contribution is often of such a highly specialized nature that much of it necessarily must lie beyond his range of comprehension. Indeed, from the work of writers of the twentieth century it would be difficult to infer that they were living in an age of science triumphant.[3]

What they reacted to were the philosophical implications of science. They understood that thoroughgoing revisions had to be made in the Cartesian system of reducing all phenomena to sense-data and Newton's mechanical model of the universe. Einstein's mathematical formulas upset the universality of the laws of gravitation. The element of time brought unforeseen complications into the cause-and-effect sequence. Tiny particles could not be measured to determine their future position. Nature, informed with a principle of uncertainty, suddenly ceased to be a gigantic mechanism. Not that the principle of indeterminacy undermined the validity of the scientific world. Science still enables us to predict the future on the basis of our present knowledge, but it cannot furnish us with conclusions that are universally true. Though cause and effect still apply to operations on a large scale, the idea of cause has been replaced by that of chance. Science, which functions in a world that is ever changing, is not dealing with absolutes, but the truth of determinism is still tested by the degree of accuracy with which it forecasts events that have not yet taken place. Science, in short, remains the standard by which all things must be measured.

This is the brave new world as science pictures it, a relativized, chancy, uncertain, and yet "determined" world. Step by step, science teaches man to cast off his previous dependence on nature. And yet, it is science which has reduced man to utter insignificance in the universe.[4] He dwells in a technological age that is bewilderingly specialized. He is assured that the time is not far distant when machines will do all his necessary work for him while he simply attends to the easy task of supervision. Oddly enough, this vision of utopian felicity fills many with dismay, for what is man to do with himself and his blessed gift of leisure? What ultimate purpose will make his life meaningful and rewarding? What is he to live *for*? It was this vision of the socialist paradise, without benefit of God, that Dostoevski inveighed against. Man does not live by bread alone. "If man had no spiritual life, no ideal of Beauty," Dostoevski warned, "he would fall into a state of depression, he would die, he would become insane, he would commit suicide."[5]

But the mighty advance of science was not to be halted. In its effort to fit all empirical phenomena within the framework of "law," the scientific method progressively substituted analysis for intuition, logic for feeling. The entire cosmos was split into atoms and then electrons. The sun was a mass of flaming gas, water became a chemical formula, the greenness of grass was caused by the chlorophyll it contained. "Spirit" was a metaphor without meaning; only the body exists: blood, cells, nerves, brain, stomach, glandular secretions, conditioned reflexes. According to logical positivism, ethical judgments make assertions that have no bearing on reality.[6] And aesthetics is merely a discipline designed to express certain feelings and call forth certain responses.[7] It was this gross simplification of human experience that triggered the literary revolt against science and the myth that it was the sole mediator of reality. The difficult problem these insurgent writers faced was that of bridging the gulf between the world of science with its abstractions and mathematical formulas and the world of psychological time and space. The mechanical man is not the man of flesh and blood. The ghostly universe fathered by science is not the reality that is created and experienced by human perceptions.

Largely abandoned today is the faith held in the nineteenth century by men like Renan, Comte, Zola, Taine, and Thomas Henry Huxley that science could solve all problems. Though it is still cherished by a dramatist like Brecht and a psychologist turned didactic novelist like Skinner, modern literature is throwing off the spell cast by scientism. Though the world is still governed by the scientific method, the dangers and limitations of science are now all too apparent. The scientist, both savior and diabolist, has demonstrated that everything is subject to change. Our knowledge of reality is only partially reliable. The world changes and our interpretation of it changes. For that matter, nature alters its appearance as we see it from different points of view. Here was the insight that dethroned the myth of "objectivity." The scientific mind had to adapt itself to reality by ending the reign of the absolute and setting up in its place the concept of relativity: not only the relativity of time and space, but also the relativity of reason, logic, truth, and even science itself. Hence "it follows that the notions of truth and of evidence are eminently subjective, and that, even within the framework of science. The error lies, to our mind, in thinking there is only one reality, whereas there are several, according to the individual or group taking cognizance of them."[8]

This transvaluation of values was prefigured in the work of Nietzsche, the prophet of relativism. In *Joyful Wisdom*, published in 1882 (though the fifth book was added in 1886), he broadcasts the glad tidings that unto man is granted the fullness of life and the fullness of eternity. Man must give up the pursuit of the absolute. Evertyhing must be brought into question, even the presupposition that truth exists. Nietzsche derived a quasireligious ecstasy from embracing the doctrine of eternal recurrence, but if every truth was to be challenged, then this mystical but nihilistic "truth," too, was suspect. Science forbade the honest and intrepid thinker from cherishing fixed convictions. He must be free to experiment with as-if fictions. Science required an attitude of uncompromising skepticism, though this requirement is in itself based on a premise about the nature of truth. Nietzsche clairvoyantly stated the epistemological paradox that bedevils the literary mind today:

One sees that science also rests on a belief: there is no science at all "without premises." The question whether *truth* is necessary, must not merely be affirmed beforehand, but must be affirmed to such an extent that the principle, belief, or conviction finds expression, that "there is nothing *more necessary* than truth, and in comparison with it everything else has only secondary value."—The absolute will to truth: what is it? Is it the will *not to allow ourselves to be deceived*? For the will to truth could also be interpreted in this fashion, provided one included under the generalisation, "I will not deceive," the special case, "I will not deceive myself." But why not deceive? Why not allow oneself to be deceived?[9]

The will to truth, as Nietzsche iconoclastically suggests, may be a disguised form of the will to death.[10] But what if this will to truth is itself mistaken?

This is the problem the writers of our time have had to wrestle with: reality versus illusion, truth as opposed to as-if fictions. The excesses of rationalism called forth an idealistic reaction against the hegemony of science. Bergson led the attack by insisting that the living organism cannot be properly apprehended by laws applicable to things. Those poets, novelists, and critics who challenged the claims to absolute truth on the part of science argued that the imagination, far from being a hindrance to our interpretation of reality, is an integral part of all our experience, the condition that underlies all perception. Whereas the scientist asks no questions that cannot be empirically answered, the creative vision of the artist takes in a different and much wider universe of perception, rejecting nothing in the domain of human experience: dreams, fantasies, the irrational, subjective choice. Though numerous works have appeared which seek to reconcile literature and science (H. J. Muller's *Science and Criticism*, Martin Johnson's *Art and Scientific Thought*, Harold Gomes Cassidy's *The Sciences and the Arts*), it is extremely doubtful that the opposition between science and the literary arts can be overcome. What science, with its rigorous devotion to propositional truth, dismisses as error, literature welcomes under the heading of "illusion."[11]

2. THE LITERARY REVOLT AGAINST SCIENCE

When writers turn against what they consider the tyranny of science, they are not presumptuous enough, even if they are sufficiently knowledgeable, to attack science on its own grounds. For then the contest would be absurdly unequal: the slim David of ignorance, armed with a slingshot of invectives, pitted against the Goliath of science. No, what the modern writer assails is the right of science to speak for him in matters where it clearly has no authority. He will not be cheated of his "truths" and "myths," however relative and vulnerable these prove to be. He is convinced that whatever secrets science can wrest from nature, it cannot grasp the secret of the creative energy alive in the universe and active in the heart and mind of man. Such is the extraordinary power and prestige of science that he cannot afford to ignore it, though he modifies it to suit his own needs, rejecting what he considers false or unwarranted in its outlook.

In *Back to Methuselah*, Shaw, a rationalist who attacked many of the sacred cows of science, replaced Darwinism with his own brand of creative evolution. A more concentrated attack on science was made by D. H. Lawrence.[12] He rejected the Freudian system and its clinical analysis of the unconscious. He was revolted by the doctrine of psychic determinism. Instead of making man more genuinely unself-conscious, spontaneous, instinctive—and the artist needed to be that if his creative powers were not to be stifled—psychoanalysis turned him into a peeping Tom of the psychic underworld. When D. H. Lawrence declared war against the science of psychoanalysis, he knew what he was doing: he was protecting his personality against the forces which he believed made for disintegration. The mind was not a cadaver to be dissected. In his poetry and fiction he voiced his new-won faith in the passional consciousness, in "the knowledge" that flows in the bloodstream. If he looked for revelations, it was not by means of surrealist conjuring tricks, psychic automatism, or by drugging his unconscious. The artist, he maintained, had to be alone, self-contained, fixed in his earth-rooted identity. He had, in addition, to establish an instinctive relationship with the cosmos and rise above the fenced-in limits imposed by the scientists. If he extravagantly admired the primitives, it was because they lived in rapport with the cosmos and knew its splendor and power. They actually beheld the glory of the sun, not the scientifically refracted body of flaming gas that modern man thinks he sees. D. H. Lawrence declares with passion:

The sun has a great blazing consciousness, and I have a little blazing consciousness. When I can strip myself of the trash of personal feelings and ideas, and get down to my naked sun-self, then the sun and I can commune by the hour, the blazing interchange, and he gives me life, sun-like, and I send him a little new brightness from the world of the bright blood.[13]

In his determination to commune with cosmic reality, Lawrence writes what may sound like arrant nonsense, but he is using the symbolic language spoken by primitive man and by the Hebraic prophets of old. He has no need to "prove" his point that there is a vital correspondence between his blood and the sun. He feels it, he experiences it, and for him it becomes a living truth. That is what he would do: restore the power of myth, recapture the vitality of symbolic forms.

If we get out of contact and harmony with the sun and moon, then both turn into great dragons of destruction against us. The sun is a great source of blood-vitality, it streams strength through us. But once we resist the sun, and say: It is a mere ball of gas!—then the very streaming vitality of sunshine turns into subtle disintegrative force in us, and undoes us.[14]

Cut off from nature, the Mother of all that is instinct with life, man turns neurasthenic. Lawrence, the poet and mystic, knows the cure for this sickness of spirit. Instead of being dominated by the cult of rational efficiency and scientific coordination, man must rely on his intuitions. Life is its own justification and reward. Lawrence longed to reinstate the ancient modes of consciousness, the ability to perceive the inherent mystery of things. Everything in the universe is alive, filled with godhood. Lawrence would have become one with nature. Here, as one religious critic remarks, is animism revived, "nature-worship, life-worship, power-worship, fertility cult, magic, in full bloom."[15]

D. H. Lawrence is no fool. If, like Dostoevski's underground man, he combats the aggressive spirit of rationalism, he is under no misapprehension that he is in any meaningful sense refuting the theories of science. He is simply asserting the autonomy of the creative imagination, the right of the poet to rule in his own demesne. Like Wordsworth, he would rather be a pagan suckled in a creed outworn so that he might have sight of Proteus rising from the sea, except that for him the creed was not outworn. It was, or he tried to make it become, very much alive. Just as Whitman, in "When I Heard the Learn'd Astronomer," recovered from the experience of listening to a lecture replete with figures, charts, and diagrams by going out into the night, wandering off by himself, and looking up in silence at the stars, so Lawrence affirms the truth of his mystical vision of reality by rejecting the abstract laws and principles of science. In his poem, "Anaxagoras," he takes his fling at the scientists' refusal to accept the testimony of the senses. As a poet Lawrence fulminates against the forces that would turn everything into a mechanism. He holds up the robot as the symbol of evil. Science is the enemy to be defeated. The intellect is the supreme danger, the foe of life. Mindlessness is salvation. He could not tolerate "the idea of fixed, mechanical law, the 'bunk of geology, and strata, and . . . biology or evolution,' or the substitution of H_2O for the naive, potable element."[16]

Hence his interest, as we shall see in the following chapter, in the fruitfulness of myth, the potency of archetypal symbols that are precognitive, belonging to the primordial rhythm of the blood. His great religion—and he was in his way a profoundly religious man—rested on "a belief in the blood, the flesh, as being wiser than the intellect. We can go wrong in our minds. But what our blood feels and believes and says, is always true. The intellect is only a bit and bridle. What do I care about knowledge?"[17] This is nonsense of course, but it is creative nonsense that is highly revealing and affirms its own kind of poetic truth. It is designed to exalt the function of the artist. As a novelist, Lawrence considers himself superior to the philosopher and the scientist, not to mention the saint.[18] As a novelist he deals with the live man, the whole man, and not with the separate parts. There is, however, no absolute in his portrayal of man. "We should ask for no absolutes, or absolute. Once and for all and for ever, let us have done with the ugly imperialism of any absolute. There is no absolute good, there is nothing absolutely right. All things flow and change, and even change is not absolute."[19]

Though Lawrence is here repudiating all absolutes, he is by no means reconciled to the scientific outlook. For him the aim of life is not to know but to *be*. Life has become intellectualized and that is death to the creative spirit. The trouble with modern man is that he has permitted the idea to replace the autonomous life of impulse; he does not act spontaneously and out of a sense of wholeness. Life, Lawrence insists, is always individual, and nothing else. Why should he give credence to the theories of science? The only valid clue to the universe is to be found not in scientific speculation but in the life of the individual. Using nature as his key metaphor, Lawrence will not deny the body and its own, the source of all that is most precious and beautiful in man. He refuses to believe that the body and mind are mechanisms controlled by heredity and determinism. He is not prepared to sacrifice the vital, creative truths he lives by for the abstract and therefore sterile conclusions of science. Whatever progress science may make, he is convinced that it will never solve the mystery of existence.

Lawrence would seem to be deepening the cleavage between the two cultures by denouncing the scientists as a race of barbarians who are blind to the humanistic wisdom of the past and indifferent, if not hostile, to the power of art. Taken aback by these intemperate charges, the scientists, for their part, begin to suspect that literary men, by and large, are idealistic idiots and ignorant dilettantes. C. P. Snow, who is himself a novelist, calmly rebuts the accusation that scientists are lacking in vision. They are not removed from the human condition; their involvement in life, like that of all men, is inescapably tragic; each one works and lives alone and dies alone. The only difference is that the scientist, unlike the literary nihilist, refuses to lie down and give up the ghost right there and then; he labors to improve the aspects of life that can be improved. If the scientists are impoverished by their failure to derive some benefit from the literary culture, the literary brethren are impoverishing themselves in turn by culpably neglecting to acquaint themselves with the scientific culture, "as though the scientific edifice of the physical world was not, in its intellectual depth, complexity, and articulation, the most beautiful and wonderful collective work of the mind of man."[20]

The literary men do not deny the Promethean character of the scientific enterprise. They do not actually believe that the scientists are engaged in a dastardly conspiracy to mechanize and eventually to destroy civilization. They know that when the scientist steps out of his field of specialization and stops to consider the issue of the ultimate he finds himself caught in a metaphysical impasse. The scientist must then invoke values which science can neither provide nor validate. He must, by his own reckoning, face up to the implications of entropy, the vision of a world dying. Life may be a comparatively rare phenomenon confined to a limited stretch of time, and a period may come, perhaps not far distant, when all life on this planet will cease. If all life is bound to come to a disastrous end, then how is the scientist to live his life? Norbert Wiener, one of the leaders in the development of cybernetics, acknowledges that the human environment must be interpreted in terms of human values. "There is a very true sense in which we are shipwrecked passengers on a doomed planet. Yet even in a shipwreck, human decencies and human values do not necessarily all vanish, and we must make the most of them. We shall go down, but let it be in a manner to which we may look forward as worthy of our dignity."[21]

The battle, today as in the past, is over the question of values. There is no reason why the leading representatives of the two cultures cannot treat each other with respect, but it is difficult to see how they can be reconciled. From the point of view of the imaginative writer, the scientific synthesis is mistaken in its interpretation of human nature. The truth about man cannot be comprehended within an empirical framework; such an approach transforms him into a thing. The existential nature of man cannot be summed up in any definition, not even in a scientific definition.

What Lawrence protested against was the attempt to dissipate the mystery of being by treating man as if he were a machine. The mystique of the objective cuts man off from nature; the split between subject and object is widened. Modern Western culture, extroverted and dynamic, pays little attention to the cosmic dimension, the timeless order of events. But man is part of nature and cannot get out of it. If, as Lawrence holds, the only goal of life is life itself, then the present, far from being an illusion to be transcended perpetually for the sake of some future utopian consummation, is the essence of the real. In his opposition to the scientific perspective, Lawrence struggled to celebrate life by recovering the power of the mythic consciousness.

1. GENERAL CONSIDERATIONS

IT IS NOT surprising that in an age of scientific and technological specialization a number of writers are making a determined effort to recapture the method—and incidentally the benefits—of mythical thinking. The products of the mythical imagination are no longer regarded as a species of primitive superstition, but as an intuitive way of interpreting and responding to the world. What the mythical consciousness discloses is what every post-Einsteinian poet discovers for himself: namely, that there is no such thing as a pure or absolute phenomenal reality. The primitive mind confronts a reality that has already been transformed creatively by the mythopoeic process. Not even the scientist ever beholds nature in its essential objectivity, whatever that might be, but always as shaped and colored by the mind. Euclid alone, according to Edna St. Vincent Millay, has looked on Beauty bare, but what of that? Nature perversely resists being reduced to a set of mathematical symbols.

The original myths were not quests for knowledge, rudimentary struggles to conquer reality by dint of intellectual analysis; they served vastly more than a cognitive function. They represented one vital and important dimension of human consciousness. The myth, which grows out of necessity, is lived and develops its own sense of reality. It is not an "escape" into a magical world of make-believe. It is not something to be apprehended conceptually and then believed. It constitutes the heart of "objective" reality to those people who believed in it because they lived it. In the world of myth, as in the work of art, all things endure in an eternal present, on a single plane of reality that is mediated by the sensuous image, so that dream and reality are not differentiated. Hence for the myth-haunted mind of primitive man drama was ritual, not an abstract aesthetic but a form of sacred action. In this world-view, word and name magic "are, like image magic, an integral part of the magical world view. But in all this the basic presupposition is that word and name do not merely have a function of describing or portraying but contain within them the object and its real powers."[1]

The difficult question for the modern writer is this: if mythical vision pervades the whole universe of perception, how can it be recovered today in its original purity? How can this primary and ultimate mystery be shared by a consciousness that has, in the course of centuries of civilization, been highly rationalized? In 1916, dadaism, revolting against contemporary society and the cult of mechanical progress that culminated in the First World War, experimented with nonsense, nursery rhymes, and poems of absolute sound. Rejecting the norms as well as the language of logic, the leaders of this movement invoked the mythic forces of chance and instinct.[2] But the significant poetry and art to which dada gave birth for the brief period of its existence could not root itself in the soil of some myth which could unify the world of experience. Dada was destructive in its aim, whereas the myths of the primitive world stressed the theme of eternal life, always life!

As Ernst Cassirer points out in *Language and Myth*, what the mythical consciousness beholds in its contemplation of the stars is radically different from the spectacle the stars present "to empirical observation or the way they figure in theoretical speculation and scientific 'explanations' of natural phenomena."[3] The myth is thus a welcome corrective to the limitations imposed by scientific rationalism. Blake, long before D. H. Lawrence, decried the Newtonian metaphor of a mechanical universe as spelling death to the divine poetic imagination. He insisted on having a universe that was responsive to his creative needs, one in which, as Mark Schorer says, "all things were in organic and active relationship with all others."[4] As Lawrence fiercely protested, the principle of causality rules the mind of modern man as an absolute, with the result that determinism not only strips him of his sense of freedom but makes him feel utterly cut off from nature and its recurrent miracles of novelty. Reaction against this in part accounts for the resurgence of myth and the high esteem in which it is held today.

But the realization that beyond the scientific cosmology of matter and energy there is the universe of the contingent and the inexplicable is not enough to reinstate the mythic consciousness in its pristine freshness. The Greek tragic writers neither sought for nor questioned myth; they used it. To Sophocles, myth is life, with all its burden of sorrow and impenetrable mystery.[5] Sophocles provides no answers; he dramatically projects the vital substance of the myth and his audience must make of it what they can. The meaning incorporated in myth is not susceptible of rational explanation, and in this it resembles poetry or an authentic work of art. It cannot be translated into other terms.

The age of myth can only be reconstructed by a tremendous effort of the historical intellect or by an imaginative process of empathy. Conditioned by science, the modern creative sensibility finds it extremely difficult, if not impossible, to draw nourishment and inspiration from mythopoeic sources. A metaphorically alive universe, peopled with gods and spirits, is no longer believable in a world of relativity, nuclear physics, and non-Euclidian geometry. This, paradoxically enough, helps us to understand why some writers today desperately cast about for new redemptive myths, though most of them go about it the wrong way. Myth, like faith, cannot be won by the maieutic force of desire. Lawrence, who strove mightily to regain the lost cosmic consciousness of primitive man, declares:

The cosmos is a vast living body, of which we are still parts. The sun is a great heart whose tremors run through our smallest veins. The moon is a great gleaming nerve-centre from which we quiver forever. Who knows the power that Saturn has over us, or Venus? But it is a vital power, rippling exquisitely through us *all the time.* And if we deny Aldebaran, Aldebaran will pierce us with infinite dagger-thrusts. He who is not with me is against me!—that is a cosmic law.

Now all this is *literally* true, as men knew in the great past, and as they will know again.[6]

It may have been true in the remote past but it is exceedingly doubtful if modern men will again "know" this truth. They will be pierced to the heart by Aldebaran; they will suffer the full consequences of this deprivation. As Lawrence himself realized, the overdeveloped consciousness of modern man prevents him from responding instinctively to the sun and the moon and the stars. True myth is a spontaneous relationship to the cosmos. It is "a belief unconsciously held, and we have been hyper-conscious about the poet's need for myth."[7] The past four centuries have given rise to a powerful current of skepticism that militates effectually against the ancient world of myth. The face of the universe is unveiled, progressively shorn of mystery, whereas there is no myth "which is not the unveiling of a 'mystery.' "[8] Collective in content and universal in meaning, myth transcends the here and now, the sphere of the profane and the secular. It therefore follows that myths cannot be brought into the modern world by force majeure, even though this world betrays disguised traces of mythic consciousness at work. The mystique of the revolutionary proletariat that Sorel describes in *Reflections on Violence* and the Marxist vision of the classless society both have their roots in the dream of the Golden Age. Thus, though the myth seems to die in modern times, it never altogether passes from the scene; it simply persists in different and debased forms.

The old myths are historical relics; the religious meanings which they embody can no longer be seriously accepted. The writer is consequently forced, like Yeats, to invent his own myths. The crisis of the modern mind is its alienation from ancient sources of myth and its inability to sink its roots deep into the substratum of some new vivifying myth. A culture that has lost its mythic consciousness has also lost its power of creativity. Nietzsche pictures for us the pathetic spectacle of modern man, denied the fecundating gift of myth, frantically trying to recapture it by digging among the ruins of the past. "What does our great historical hunger signify, our consuming desire for knowledge, if not the loss of myth, of a mythic home, the mythic womb?"[9] Each age sees a further disintegration of mythology; the myths of Greece are discredited by the triumph of Christianity, and then the biblical myths are themselves overthrown.

That is the grievous handicap under which the twentieth-century writer must labor. His effort to create new myths or archetypal characters who will be the bearers of these myths seems foredoomed to failure. Figures like Stephen Dedalus and Leopold Bloom are not really mythological characters. As Hermann Broch, the author of the metaphysical novel, *The Sleepwalkers*, declares, the modern myth,

> which so many poets are eager to create, does not exist; there exists only something which could actually be described as counter-myth: myth, after all, is cosmogony, is description of those primordial powers which menace and destroy man, and oppose their symbolic figures with hero-symbols no less promethean, which reveal how man conquers the apparently unconquerable and is capable of living on earth. None of this is still pertinent today, or rather, mythological rationality has been superseded by the scientific rationality.[10]

Modern man seeks to defeat the primeval powers by spinning new myths, intellectualizing what was originally an instinctive and unconscious process. But the more civilized the life of man becomes, "the more he wants to return to the primitive in theory. . . . Thus the present popularity of the myth corresponds to a collective need rather than a romantic infatuation."[11] D. H. Lawrence, the prophetic voice of our age, sought to give expression to a vision of reality that is personalized and alive. How much of this vision came through?

2. MYTH IN LAWRENCE'S FICTION

Lawrence toward the end of his life believed devoutly in the principle of *mana*, the charismatic power of the great personality that makes itself felt like the efflux of light from the sun. Also important in shaping his aesthetic values and influencing his interpretation of reality was his awareness of the night side of the self. That is what he meant when he glorified the blood-consciousness as the source of all that is best and most original in man. It is this sensual, instinctive, organic self which he hoped would serve as the foundation stone of the new society. The new man, reborn, will be concerned not with the counters of conceptual knowledge but with the living truth of his own experience, the evidence communicated by his five senses. Lawrence refused to accept as valid a mechanistic physiology which looked upon the marvelously integrated body of man as made of so many glands, ganglia, and reflexes. No, the vital spark comes first, the inextinguishable soul of life, and the soul is present even if it cannot be defined. This mysterious entity is the individual self which no mechanistic theory can explain.

If Lawrence denounced science as a form of death, he was aware of the equally great danger of an idealism and spirituality which suppressed the sensual self. In his anti-intellectualism, he frequently made statements which sound like paradoxes:

The supreme lesson of human consciousness is to learn how *not to know*. That is, how not to *interfere*. That is, how to live dynamically, from the great Source, and not statically, like machines driven by ideas and principles from the head.[12]

Modern man is cursed by the tendency to intellectualize his whole world of experience.

In his works Lawrence set himself in opposition to what he considered the great danger of his age: the intellectualization of life and art. But the vehemence with which he exalted the sacredness of the individual self showed that he was himself the victim of alienation, a problem which never troubled the mind of primitive man, rigidly bound to his community by custom and tradition.[13] An arch-individualist, Lawrence strove to liberate himself from the clutches of his possessive ego, to establish genuine contact with other men and thus break out of his isolation. He had to find some way of imbuing his work with a sense of social responsibility, to heal the breach between art and society, self and community. Recurrently, in his letters as well as in his poetry and fiction, he describes his horror of the strictly personal element. Though this personal element is actually his chief source of strength as a writer, it fills him again and again with a feeling of guilt. He desired to engage in some nonpersonal activity, to institute relations which are based upon "some unanimous accord in truth or belief, and a harmony of purpose. . . . I am sick of personality."[14]

Like most of his contemporaries, Lawrence could rely on no collective myth to sustain him. He was not in the least attracted by socialism. If it were not held in check, he warned, it would prove the nemesis of civilization, reducing life to its lowest common denominator. He could not afford to sacrifice his individuality. The gospel he preached is that of primitive anarchism, the path to a genuine organic relationship to the universe. This metaphysical rather than mythic urge stirred in him as he endeavored to combat the collectivistic manias of his age. But he knew, too, that if he followed strictly the bidding of desire as the supreme law of his being (he used the term "God" as synonymous with his desire),[15] he was in effect separating himself from the great body of humanity. He had at all costs to be himself, but to be himself was not enough. What ailed him, as he confessed, was "the absolute frustration of my primeval societal instinct."[16] He was, he said, "weary even of my own individuality, and simply nauseated by other people's."[17] In the end he celebrated the natural power of greatness resident in some men. Hence his fulminations, in *Apocalypse*, against revolutionary as well as religious saints who deny "the natural proud self of power."[18]

Lawrence was a divided man until the end of his days, worn out by this conflict between untrammeled individuality and the need to be part of some transcendent social purpose. On the one hand, he jealously guarded the sacredness of his individuality and on the other he detested modern man because he personalized everything in the universe, situating his ego in the center of the cosmos. Lawrence tried to resolve the conflict by emulating the example of the pagans. He invoked the image of man as visceral rather than cerebral, a living mystery that is fused and flows with the cosmic stream of energy. It is this primal sense of mystery, the mythic perspective, that Lawrence labored to restore. Over and over again, he stressed the urgent need for man to plant himself in his deeper instinctive self, to heed the voice of his dreams and the call of his blood. As he proclaimed in *Apocalypse*, man could come back to his integral and unique self only by realizing that he is the creative fountainhead of the universe. This faith in individualism is one of the major reasons why Lawrence turned against those systems of thought that made the collectivity dominant at the expense of the individual. He searched eagerly for some spot on earth where he could found an ideal community, but none of the projects he was enthusiastic about ever came to fruition. If he celebrated the primacy of the blood-consciousness, he did so in order to protest against all attempts to control the mind as if it were a rational machine or to "condition" the individual as if he were nothing more than a cell in the social organism. His creative work as a whole represented a heroic quest for the authenticity of being.

This quest, he perceived, could never take a fixed form, for it was essentially indefinable, a plunge into the dark unfathomable heart of the universe. Each one must obey the god within—that is the saving motif to be found in his fiction.[19] The individual is the supreme fact. To capture this secret of integral selfhood, one must have the courage to become what he is, regardless of conventional moral standards or institutional ideals. Lawrence's hero, when the chips are down, will not submit to the dictates of society.

In *The Rainbow*, Lawrence portrays love as the central mystery, a process of awakening and fulfillment, the human rediscovery of the mysterious pattern that works itself out in nature, in clod and plant and animal, except that human beings fight against the power of love and try to live solely by the intellect. Love is a struggle in which two bodies and two wills wrestle for mastery, a conflict in which one or the other of the human pair is consumed, until they recognize each other as separate and different yet fused and interdependent in the blood. Lawrence traces Ursula's spiritual growth with profound sympathy and insight. She rebels against the dogmas of Christianity; she perceives the threat posed by the dehumanizing power of the machine. She is aware of the outer darkness which does not include civilization and science and industrialism nor marriage and the family of man. Always she feels around her the infinite, primordial dark that reduces the world of light to utter nothingness. She is overcome by a numinous vision of the incomprehensible mystery of life. "It was a consummation, a being infinite. She was a oneness with the infinite. To be oneself was a supreme, gleaming triumph of infinity."[20] Skrebensky, her lover, who is caught up in the established order of things, cannot hold her.

The story of her quest for fulfillment in love and life is resumed in *Women in Love*. It is Birkin who, in *Women in Love*, formulates Lawrence's faith in pure sensuality, "the great dark knowledge you can't have in your head—the dark involuntary being."[21] Like Aaron and Lilly in *Aaron's Rod*, he is trying to break away from socially imposed standards, to respond to his deepest instincts. He voices a primitivism that reaches out for the blood-consciousness of the ancient man of myth. Civilization, in its idealization of love, is fathering a lie; love is merely one of the emotions, Birkin argues, and should not be made an absolute. He cannot surrender himself to abstractions like humanity or brotherhood. In an ultimate sense, one is alone, and the sentiment of love cannot help a man overcome this cosmic loneliness. He wants to be united with Ursula on the plane of the impersonal, without obligations or commitments, he desires the primal, unconscious self of Ursula in a union of love that does not minister to egoism. Partly through him, Ursula comes to the knowlege that the body is only one of the manifestations of spirit. Man is not the measure of the universe. If man cannot keep up, he will be left behind, but the eternal mystery of creation and renewal will go on. "To be man was as nothing compared to the possibilities of the creative mystery."[22]

Lawrence is perpetually in search of the ultimate secret, the creative mystery of the self. This secret could be found if the body and mind submitted to the elemental powers of nature. This mythic pattern of death and rebirth he tried to symbolize in his novels and much of his poetry. In *Aaron's Rod* he repeated the theme that there is no goal outside the self. One can only be as big as the self inside him. Destiny comes from within, and cannot be scientifically dissected or known in advance. Lawrence hoped, of course, that his work would help bring about this return to organic health and wholeness. He would dig deeper into the rich subsoil of consciousness and reveal the aspects of being that discursive language was incapable of dealing with. From the beginning of his correspondence with Bertrand Russell, we can see the conflict between the intuitive personality and the rationalist. The prophet of a mystical irrationalism, the lyricist of the chthonic instincts, Lawrence wanted very much to rise above the sterile abstractions of the mind and, by doing so, to enhance and intensify the quality of life. He wrote Russell on December 8, 1915 (the year in which *The Rainbow* was published), after reading Frazer's *The Golden Bough* and *Totemism and Exogamy*: "Now I am convinced of what I believed when I was about twenty—that there is another seat of consciousness than the brain and the nerve system: there is a blood-consciousness which exists in us independently of the ordinary mental consciousness."[23] Lawrence was in dead earnest when he insisted that the mental consciousness must not be permitted—as was the case, he charged, with Bertrand Russell—to tyrannize over the blood-consciousness.

While living in New Mexico, Lawrence felt a profound sympathy for the pagan gods. In the desert at the foot of the Rockies he became convinced that the concept of one god will not do, especially when he sat with the Indians around the leaping fire listening to their tribal songs till far into the night, and joined with them in the earthy rhythm of the Indian dance. Under the combined influence of desert and dance, night and the stars and the hypnotic spell of the song chanted in unison, he could overcome the European metaphysical obsession, the delirious quest for unity. How can all these civilizations and cultures, these multitudinous religions and gods be unified, and to what end? "No more unison among man than among the wild animals—coyotes and chipmunks and porcupines and deer and rattlesnakes. They all lived in these hills—in the unison of avoiding one another. As for *willing* the world into better shape—better chaos a thousand times than any 'perfect' world."[24] Lawrence was gravitating steadily in the direction of myth, but his experiments in myth represented an attempt to utilize intuitions and instincts for a creative purpose.

The Plumed Serpent (1926) is a *willed* sortie in myth, a magnificent tour de force. With strident iteration Lawrence proclaims his faith in the new god and the new religion. Mexico provides the sultry, apocalyptic background of faith and myth, but it remains largely colorful background, just as the main characters are largely mouthpieces for the evangel of salvation to be attained through fusion with mother earth. The novel imaginatively promulgates the vision of life Lawrence then beheld: the need for man to make a fresh start. The Mexican savior and anti-Christ holds up an image of life, pure and intense, which puts to shame the kind of devitalized existence Europeans lead. This greater life calls for the repudiation of the gregarious pull of mankind. Kate Leslie, the American heroine, is in the process of freeing herself of the past; she is the receptive one waiting for the Word Incarnate in Man. Don Ramon, the prophet of the new faith, and Don Cipriano, his disciple, both labor to "convert" Kate. Though she resents their heathenish and absurd rituals, she is drawn at the end to the worship of their gods.

The Plumed Serpent is thick with symbols: symbols of awakening and rebirth, serpent and rain, vegetation and earth, lake and sky, drought and bullfights. Don Ramon, aided by Cipriano and his army, sets out to liberate his land and save his people. When the Roman Catholic priests rouse the mob to resist this fascist movement, Cipriano uses his armed forces to defeat them. The church is expropriated. A native religious renaissance is to be brought about by a new ritual of nature-worship. Quetzalcoatl, a composite of bird and snake, is an Aztec god who is capable of joining earth and sky, below and above, sex and spirit. Don Ramon is convinced that he is the incarnation of Quetzalcoatl; the serpent resides in his loins and the bird on his brow; he is the lord of both ways of life. Quetzalcoatl is the symbol of human aspiration, the perennial quest for perfection and renewal, the source of the ultimate mystery embodied in the morning star. Here is the god who preaches the Laurentian gospel of sex, bidding man be a man and requiring of woman that she root herself in her womanhood.

Lawrence's attack on mental consciousness and his dithyrambic descriptions of the rituals of Don Ramon seem forced. The songs, the incantations, the dances, the brooding landscape, the resurrection of Quetzalcoatl and the banishment of Jesus, all this is not far removed from melodrama. This is a "mythical" novel that somehow fails to come off. The primitive myths are not sufficiently distanced. The treatment of the theme fails to induce a willing suspension of disbelief. Using the myth as a vehicle for his perspectivism, Lawrence announces that man creates God in his own image. The old gods grow older and must die like the men who gave them birth. Fascinated by the symbol of Quetzalcoatl which stands for the Plumed Serpent, Kate Leslie reflects: "Even the gods must be born again. We must be born again."[25]

It is Don Ramon who introduces her to the idea of the return of Quetzalcoatl. He tells her it is time for Jesus to be banished to the place where the dead gods go. What Mexico suffers from is the domination of the white man's consciousness, impotent yet destructive, infected with the will to die. The only conscious people in Mexico are those of mixed blood. When Kate, secretly longing to be reborn and yet fearful of being roused out of her lethargy, asks him what is to be done, he replies: "One is driven, at last, back to the far distance, to look for God."[26] Like Lawrence, he is "nauseated with humanity and the human will."[27] Here in Mexico the deadly consciousness of the white man encounters the stubborn if inarticulate resistance of the Indian, and the white man is overcome, his white God routed.

Lawrence is composing a dirge for a dying Christianity whose death he would fain hasten. He describes the stripping of the church. The bier is carried out, on it the lifelike figure of Christ. Then comes litter after litter bearing the scourged body of Christ, the image of the Savior of the Sacred Heart, the image of Jesus with a crown of thorns, the Virgin with the golden crown. The saints, too, are borne out and finally the church is plunged in darkness. The strange procession makes its way to the lake. The men with the crucifix and the plaster images deposit them on an open ship, each image destined for the funeral pyre. Lawrence ends this symbolic act of fiery destruction with the sentence: "Sayula was empty of God."[28]

But man needs God, and Ramon reopens the church, which is now the house of Quetzalcoatl. Inside, instead of the crucified Jesus, there is a huge carved wooden figure of a naked man, "holding his right arm over his head, and on the right arm balanced a carved wooden eagle with outspread wings whose upper surface gleamed with gold, near the light, whose under surface was black shadow. Round the heavy left leg of the man-image was carved a serpent, also glimmering gold."[29] At the foot of the statue is a stone altar with a small fire burning. As the drum begins its demoniacal beat, Ramon, the living Quetzalcoatl, announces the new dispensation. There are many gods and different people must have different saviors—that is the theological perspectivism to which the novel is committed. There is one final mystery, but it assumes a multiplicity of manifestations. According to Ramon, "God must come to Mexico in a blanket and in huaraches, else He is no God of the Mexicans, they cannot know Him."[30] In a climax which is the embodiment of symbolic wish-fulfillment, Quetzalcoatl is made to triumph.

The Plumed Serpent oscillates between the two points of mystical primitivism and the apotheosis of the power of sex. It exalts blood-consciousness as a remedy for the vice of intellectualism, the curse of the machine. Sex is an expression of the divine in man, one of the ways in which the self can achieve an original relation to the universe and catch some intimations of the mystery of being. And yet, for all the fanfare of beating drums, chanted hymns, and ecstatic dances, Lawrence was fighting a losing battle. His primitivism, his cult of Quetzalcoatl, his mythic reenactment of the death and resurrection of God, his radical reconstruction of the story of the crucifixion of Christ in *The Man Who Died*, all this was meant to slay the Western god of the machine and to reveal a reality that was instinct with mystery. But Lawrence, the prophet, could not possibly succeed in his effort to utilize myth as a means of directly altering the quality of life in his age; his protests and furious polemics could not halt the wheels of progress. As George Orwell sanely points out:

When Lawrence prefers the Etruscans (*his* Etruscans) to ourselves, it is difficult not to agree with him, and yet, after all, it is a species of defeatism, because that is not the direction in which the world is moving. The kind of life that he is always pointing to, a life centering around the simple mysteries—sex, earth, fire, water, blood—is merely a lost cause. All he has been able to produce, therefore, is a wish that things would happen in a way in which they were manifestly not going to happen.[31]

Orwell is right; Lawrence must have known that the change he desired was not going to happen. He was using literature as a form of constraining magic, relying on the power of his imagination to weave a spell of myth over the mind of the reader. I am judging his work not in terms of its social effectiveness but in connection with my theme of perspectivism. Lawrence, the poetic celebrant of myth, was not concerned with propositional or empirical truth. The correctness of astrology, when compared with the science of astronomy, was, from his point of view, unimportant and irrelevant. "What we care about," Lawrence declares, "is the release of the imagination."[32] He realized full well the limitations of myth in his own time but he was convinced of its immense potentialities, since it employed images, not ideas. He was attracted to myth because it is "never an argument, it never has a didactic nor a moral purpose, you can draw no conclusion from it. Myth is an attempt to narrate a whole human experience, of which the purpose is too deep, going too deep in the blood and soul, for mental explanation or description."[33] This ineffability accounts in large measure for what is fundamentally wrong with *The Plumed Serpent*, perhaps with all modern attempts to exploit myth, as distinguished from mythological themes, in literature. The myth, born of a cosmic vision that is now dead, cannot find its objective correlative. Lawrence's novel, despite his sound conception of myth, is not only shrilly argumentative but informed with a high and passionate moral purpose. We are meant to draw some conclusion from the symbols deployed. Lawrence is trying to make language describe the unspeakable mystery of the cosmos. He is expressing his will to myth, his desire to go primitive and feel not only as the native Mexicans feel but as the Chaldeans felt when they gazed up at the stars two centuries before Christ.

He was composing a diatribe against the triumph of science, the mechanization of life, the substitution of abstractions for vital realities. He craved to return in spirit to the great ancient civilizations, which had little mathematical knowledge and were not adept at mechanical inventions. What counted, in his evaluation of a culture, was its sensitivity of feeling, its sheer vitality of being, its depth of consciousness. What he hoped to recover was the lost mystery of sense-knowledge, the mythic vision which the ancients, born poets, possessed without having to strain for it. In their response to reality they had not become victims of the ratiocinative method, whereas modern man is intellectually more complex but deficient in feeling. The latter has lost the beauty of the concrete, the vision of God shining in and through all things. The cosmos has perished, Lawrence laments, because of the rise of the scientific spirit. What he wanted at bottom was to reestablish "the living organic connections, with the cosmos, the sun and earth, with mankind and nation and family. Start with the sun, and the rest will slowly, slowly happen."[34] It was not to be, not in his lifetime.

When the current myths are found wanting and the ancient myths cannot be revived, the modern writer is at a loss where to turn. He can, like T. S. Eliot and others, find a way out of the waste land by taking the leap into faith. Those writers, however, who accept the scientific vision of the universe are often driven to adopt a suicidal skepticism. Some fall into a nihilism that is a philosophical countermyth destructive of all myths. One of the most curious perspectives that modern literature presents, and the last one that I shall deal with, is that of a nihilism which militantly justifies its rejection of life and then virtually nullifies its position by palming itself off as a doctrine of salvation. This is the paradox that inheres in the Buddhist dream of Nirvana; it is evident, too, in Schopenhauer's pessimism that recommends ways of conquering the all-powerful will to live, as if the idea, born of the will, could turn against and defeat its omnipotent begetter.

> *It is my personal feeling that the concepts of the moral world, of God and Devil, will not be abandoned altogether in the centuries to come but will gradually be rephrased and shaded in consonance with our modern scientific knowledge of the physical world. After all, Dante's poetic codification of medieval science and its synthesis with Christian theology came 1500 years after the poetic codification by Lucretius of pagan untheological science. We should then restrain our modern impatience and wait for another 1500 years for the poetic language to mature that would furnish adequate instruments for the expression of the scientific world-picture of Einstein and Curie and the religious implications this may have.*
>
> —LEO SPITZER

1. PRELUDE

LEO SPITZER may be correct in his prophecy: the womb of history may in the course of another millennium and a half give birth to strange and surprising reversals of vision, the discovery that the scientific world-picture of Einstein has profound religious implications.[1] But the nihilist who lives in the present age, dominated by the scientific synthesis, does not think so. He follows Nietzsche in declaring that God is dead and, like Nietzsche, he proves in practice to be an evangelist *manqué*, the prophet of a radically negative theology. He is disguised as a missionary, laboring to wean man away from the pernicious illusion of the divine. Even the devil suffers the fate of extinction because people no longer believe in him. In *The Death of Satan*, a recent comedy by Ronald Duncan, we are shown why Satan must perish in his own hell: disbelief is the death of him. Satan frustratedly declares: "Now faith has withered on earth, I must perish here in Hell."[2] It is in the context of this irreligious climate of thought that we must examine Jeffers's anomalous perspective of Inhumanism. Like Schopenhauer, he dedicates himself with inverted religious zeal to the task of freeing the race of men from their attachment to the wheel of suffering. His poetry, charged with this moral purpose, inevitably transforms his conception of reality.

In the West, disillusionment with the human adventure is caused chiefly by the progressive loss of religious faith in the twentieth century and the corresponding rise to power of the scientific spirit. Sons of Nietzsche, the literary nihilists find no purpose on earth worth striving for; they broadcast, often with passionate intensity of conviction, their belief (for them it is "the truth") that the world is meaningless. But their will to truth lands them in a morass of contradictions. For this will to truth may itself be compounded of illusion. If reality is not to be known, if thought proves but "an extremely defective instrument which falsifies reality and leads us astray and deceives us,"[3] then communication is rendered impossible.

But the tide of nihilism, like the mighty progress of science, could not be halted. Like Schopenhauer and Nietzsche, Heidegger led writers to undertake a drastic reexamination of the question of the ultimate meaning of life. Modern German literature, in its evolution from naturalism to expressionism, records a desperate struggle to rise above nihilistic despair.[4] This condition of spiritual emptiness and impotence is described by Hugo von Hofmannsthal in "The Letter of Lord Chandos." Lord Chandos, a gifted Renaissance poet and scholar, confesses to Lord Bacon that he has lost completely "the ability to think or to speak of anything coherently."[5] He is essentially modern in his abhorrence for such terms as "spirit," "soul," or even "body." Language fails him; all things are confounded. His anguish grows upon him so that he comes to doubt everything. There is no connection between self and nature, between perception and the world it perceives.

This vision of the absurd paralyzes all effort because it removes the ground for hope. There is no absolute order, no ultimate value toward which to strive. The modern intellectual hero is not only opposed to the traditions and truths of the past; he is antiheroic in his attitude toward the world and above all toward himself.[6] Realistic in his confrontation of what he considers to be the truth of life, he summons forth the courage to face the Naught. The contemplation of nothingness—that is his singular and incurable obsession. He defines existence, in the Heideggerian sense, as being toward death.

The philosophy implicit in the literature of the absurd is that no point of view can be trusted, just as no values can be cherished. If death conquers at the end, and there can be no doubt on that score, then it does not make any difference, Arthur Adamov feels, what attitude toward life one adopts; all values are canceled out in the fact of death.[7] Though the absurdist debunks and demystifies reality, he knows there is no going beyond the realm of the finite. This relativism of perception and the realization of the ineffectuality of reason brings the writer to an impasse. There is nothing to say, and yet this must be said. The avant-garde dramatists voice their protest against this intolerable nihilistic conclusion by relying heavily on the method of paradox and irony.

The literature of nihilism demonstrates that the archetypal urge to find the road to salvation is not to be defeated by the knowledge that there is no such road. There must be. Every time God dies he is reborn in a new form. The principle of the relative triumphs, but the hunger for the absolute, like the religious impulse in atheistic Russia, is not abated. The dialectic of the divine, as a force that counters the image of nothingness, is double-edged: if God requires mankind in order to insure his survival, as Jung says, man needs God in order to have a transcendental ideal toward which to strive. The writer as nihilist is, if only by his dedication to art, protesting against the negative faith he theoretically espouses. The paradox of art that celebrates the *nihil* is that it denies its own premises. The artist who is *completely* convinced of the futility of existence would surely lapse into silence. If he categorically rejects life as meaningless and therefore worthless, of what avail is this game he plays with words?

2. *THE IRONIC VISION OF ROBINSON JEFFERS*

Though he is clearly committed to a number of philosophical perspectives, Jeffers is not parading as a philosopher. He is under no constraint to be logically consistent in his views; as a poet he is free to contradict himself; he is portraying a reality which is ambiguous and multifaceted. Certain clusters of imagery do emerge, however, which express his feeling that civilization, a late comer on earth, is doomed. Measured against the background of cosmic time the human adventure dwindles into insignificance. Whatever changes of mood his poetry rings, he continues to espouse a naturalistic outlook. Though aware of the limitations of science, he never questions the validity of its method or the truth of its interpretation of reality.

In his portrayal of a universe that gives no warrant for anthropomorphic conceit, he voices a total nihilism. In the second poem in *The Double Axe*, "The Inhumanist," he releases the full force of his disillusionment with all things human.[8] It is in this volume that he presents his philosophy of Inhumanism. Jeffers's spokesman, the old caretaker, questions the nature of God. Whatever this God may be, he has no interest in providing the means of happiness; he is the creator of beauty, but without any regard for the needs of humanity.

In the case of Robinson Jeffers, the absolute of nihilistic rejection finds an outlet in the counterpointed method of metaphysical irony. He emphasizes the inescapable and absurd anthropomorphism of the mind of man. Indeed, man cannot abandon his ridiculous sense of self-importance; he places himself in the center of the cosmos and makes himself the measure of all things. As he contemplates the spectacle of the inordinate vanity of the human species, Jeffers is moved to Dionysian laughter; he knows, and underscores, the utter insignificance of man. The most salutary lesson the human upstart can learn is that his suffering is without meaning; his torment is swallowed up by "the sea-mouth of mortality," "the fountain six feet down."[9] Though he lashes out at the incestuous sin of self-love in which men indulge, he holds open for them the gates of deliverance. He would liberate them from the trammels of illusion. When he counsels them to turn away from love of mankind and turn instead to love of God, he is referring to the God of nature that makes possible a welcome release from the tyranny of the biological will. He bids them give up their childish faith in immortality or in the divinity of Christ.[10]

Jeffers, as a professed Inhumanist, harps on the follies and defeats that inevitably characterize human destiny. Victory is but a passing phase in the ceaseless evolution of the universe, but this evolutionary process actually goes on without any sense of direction or purpose. Unlike Nietzsche, Jeffers does not call for the advent of the superman. Like a Buddhist, he shows men caught in the net of life, but he adds that their saviors are trapped no less than the other fish. He puts these words in the mouth of Judas:

> what a net of cruelty
> Life gasps in, inextricably involved; so that I know not what to
> pray for but annihilation
> For a blessing on life.[11]

The poet is identified with Judas, who asks the blasphemous questions that rebels against God have always asked: why must the innocent perish? Who is responsible for the injustice and pain on earth? How can all this suffering and horror be endured in silence? Does no one, Judas asks in anguish, not even God, "feel it all but I alone? My soul is dark with images, and all are dreadful."[12] Jeffers's soul, too, is dark with dreadful images of the countless miseries of existence.

He is resolved, however, not to give in to pity. He knows that men are prone to invent and then believe in grandiose fictions, and he is ruthless in trying to stamp out this weakness in himself. He will not seek solace in Christianity, socialism, or science, but he does succumb to the last infirmity of creative minds, the urge to write poetry, even though he confesses in "Love the Wild Swan" that he hated his verses. Another contradiction informs his work. Though he is convinced of the futility of the human struggle, he speaks out angrily on the crucial issues of his time. In language that is excoriating and apocalyptic, he denounces the vices of modern civilization: industrialism, the cult of progress, the recurrent saturnalias of war, the lie of religion. He does so in order to hail death as a blessed state of freedom, in which man is reabsorbed into the flaming sun, the nebulae, the heart of the electron.

In "The Tower beyond Tragedy," Jeffers voices his conception of death as deliverance. Cassandra prays to death to be transmuted into another shape, into grass or stone or air wandering free between the stars and the mountain peaks,

> but cut humanity
> Out of my being, that is the wound that festers in me,
> Not captivity, not my enemies: you will heal the earth also,
> Death, in your time.[13]

Death is the new god who can release men from the fever of existence. Death is the great healer who can cure the infection of humanity. The history of the earth moves ineluctably from dark to dark, from chaos to chaos. Consciousness is a disease, an anomaly on the part of nature. Orestes, after murdering Clytemnestra and Cassandra, learns the saving truth that man is caught in a foul mesh of desires which are turned inward. His craving for death is the expression of his having fallen in love outward.

This is the burden of the nihilistic refrain Jeffers intones in his poetry. Like the stars and the sun, humanity will finally be consumed in eternal night. Though driven by the force of sexual passion, men also remember and yearn for the primal peace of the womb and realize that death is no evil. Nothing can alter the rhythm of nature that swings from ripeness to decadence, from dust to dust. It is easy to praise the beauty of nature, but why, Jeffers asks in "Meditation on Saviors," is it obligatory for man to love humanity? Jeffers cannot, however, remain indifferent to the fate of the people whose extinction he forecasts; he cannot shut out the cries of suffering mankind. Despite his rejection of the people, these apes of Christ, and his contempt for the pitiful illusions to which they cling in order to shut out the tragic sense of life, he is unable to resolve the conflict within him between compassion and his will to truth.

This points to another contradiction in his nihilistic vision. The people for whom he harbors such a feeling of contempt are, after all, part of nature. "This people as much as the sea-granite is part of the God from whom I desire not to be fugitive."[14] He counsels his heart to repudiate both love and pity, but even if he knew the ultimate secret of peace, what should prompt him to speak? "And what could his words change?"[15] Poems, like mountains, are an integral part of a universal determinism, the same causal compulsion that runs through the cosmos. He cannot prescribe magic medicine for his ailing people. Only one thing can save them: the gift of death. Then their distress will be ended forever as they are merged in the infinite unconsciousness that is God. The only logical future for the species is extinction. Jeffers preaches a pantheism that is rooted in the belief that man is a biological accident, utterly insignificant in the play of cosmic forces. Here is further evidence that the scientific dispensation gives rise to no one philosophical attitude. It may lead to a pessimism so extreme that it regards the emergence of human life on this planet as an abysmal mistake or it may provide, as in the work of Chernyshevski, H. G. Wells, Bertold Brecht, and B. F. Skinner, what are considered empirically warranted grounds for utopianism.

Jeffers's lyrics, apart from his narrative and dramatic compositions, are for the most part the products of a brooding vision that transcends the egocentric manias of mankind. The steadfast character of nature includes not only the unalterable law of change but also the process of decay and the pointlessness of human striving. Humanity is unimportant. Even the stars, tiring of their radiance, think of silence and dream of the dark peace. Jeffers makes a sincere but unavailing effort to reconcile the antithetical principles of creation and annihilation, life and death, cruelty and compassion, illusion and truth. His Inhumanism recommends that man liberate himself from his racial introversion, abandon his all-too-human desires. It is nature that is divine, it is the physical universe that endures and remains immortal. Life is a ceaseless and purposeless torment. If life is unremitting pain, then death is a most desirable consummation.

With a lyrical eloquence that reaches a pitch of veritable ecstasy, Jeffers exalts the beauty of nonbeing, the purity and impassiveness of nature as contrasted with the sadistic fury of human creatures. Though he wrote the first part of *The Double Axe and Other Poems* during the Second World War and finished the book a year before the war ended, the poems are not primarily concerned with the war.

Its burden, as of some previous work of mine, is to present a certain philosophical attitude, which might be called Inhumanism, a shifting of emphasis and significance from man to not-man; the rejection of human solipsism and recognition of the transhuman magnificence. It seems time that our race began to think as an adult does, rather than like an egocentric baby or insane person. This manner of thought and feeling is neither misanthropic nor pessimist . . . . It involves no falsehoods, and is a means of maintaining sanity in slippery times; it has objective truth and human value. It offers a reasonable detachment as a rule of conduct, instead of love, hate and envy. It neutralizes fanaticism and wild hopes; but it provides magnificence for the religious instinct, and satisfies our need to admire greatness and rejoice in beauty.[16]

Far from being pessimistic, Inhumanism, Jeffers holds, is a courageous philosophical way of facing the truth of life. It is interesting to note that, with the possible exception of Nietzsche, every relativist we have encountered insists that he is in possession of the objective truth.

"The Double Axe" is a narrative that culminates in a nightmarish climax of horror. It is an unrelieved blood-tragedy. The world Jeffers describes for us in his rage of disenchantment is "a world grown monstrous, rabies-bitten/ And nightmare-false, where millions of men are sacrificed/ For no reason but vanity, thousands of ships and great fleets of planes with crammed wombs day and night/ Labor over farthest oceans to debark death, not on armies

only,/ But old women, babies and little dogs; and worse is con-
nived at, and worse is coming."[17]

In the second part, Jeffers uses the old caretaker as a mouthpiece for his Inhumanism. The old man spends long hours brooding on the nature of God. There is no doubt that God exists: "One
energy,/ One existence, one music, one organism, one life, one
God."[18] All things have souls, but only God is immortal. Contrasted with the foulness and hellish cruelty of man is the overwhelming beauty of nature, the pure radiance of the morning star,
the majestic lift of mountains, the swooping flight of hawks, the
light of the rising sun. The members of the human race defile
whatever they touch. The caretaker envisages the time when the
sun, too, will die and the planets freeze to death. He beholds the
beasts of the Apocalypse gathering for the third world war.

I think the whole human race ought to be scrapped and is on the
        way to it; ground like fish-meal for soil-food.
What does the vast and rushing drama of the universe, seas, rocks,
        condor-winged storms, ice-fiery galaxies,
The flaming and whirling universe like a handful of gems falling down
        a dark well,
Want clowns for?[19]

The caretaker is glad that Copernicus and Darwin put man in his
place. He prefers God, the nonhuman beauty of nature, to man.
Nothing remains, he feels, but "the endless inhuman beauty of
things; even of humanity and human history/ The inhuman
beauty—and there is endurance, endurance, death's nobler
cousin."[20]

Untroubled, like Jeffers, by inconsistencies in his logic, the
old caretaker declares his faith in God—the God who will finally
settle the issue between America and Russia. "Mankind will die;
there will be no more fools; wisdom will die; the very stars will
die;/ One fierce life lasts."[21] He foresees the coming of the ice age.
Addressing the future generations, the old man says:

Trouble is coming; the world as of the present time
Sails on its rocks; but you will be born and live
Afterwards. Also a day will come when the earth
Will scratch herself and smile and rub off humanity:
But you will be born before that.
           O future children:

When you are born do not cry; it is not for long.
And when your death-day comes do not weep; you are not going far.
You are going to your better nature, the noble elements, earth, air
    and water. That's the lost paradise
The poets remember.[22]

The thing to do is to be moderately kind and give mutual help but continue to love the beauty of things, the God who is nature. In the fullness of time, God will complete his task of destruction, but whatever happens to man, nature lives on. The beauty of the cosmos is not dependent on human eyes or human consciousness. There is no remedy for the human condition except the blessedness of death.

In a later volume, *Hungerfield and Other Poems*, Jeffers reiterates his faith in the redemption to be achieved through merging with nature: "Only the acts and glory of unhuman nature or immortal God/ Can ever give our hearts peace."[23] He can discern no trace of beauty in the acts of mankind (America was then fighting a war in Korea); the acts of man are

        the acts of a sick microbe
On a satellite of a dust-grain twirled in a whirlwind
In the dust of stars . . . .
Something perhaps may come of him; in any event
He can't last long.[24]

The only thing left is "the beauty of things, not men/ The immense beauty of the world, not the human world."[25] This time he does not deny that the beauty visible in mountains and raging seas is in the eyes of the beholder, nor that man, however contemptible, is part of nature.

It is the human mind's translation of the transhuman
Intrinsic glory. It means that the world is sound,
Whatever the sick microbe does. But he too is part of it.[26]

But if he too is part of it, his only hope of salvation lies in overcoming his crazed love of life and giving up his belief in the Christian myth of redemption.

Jeffers's vision of life underwent no fundamental change as he aged. He still contrasts the immensity of sidereal space, the mighty pulsation of energy in the universe, with the introverted sickness of man. Whatever monstrous aberrations to which history will give rise, the source of energy in the nebulae will remain and perpetually renew itself. That is the secret of life's grandeur. God is energy incarnate, instinct with beauty, but indifferent to the scene of human folly. In *The Beginning and the End and Other Poems*, Jeffers again elaborates his favorite theme of the absurd insignificance of *homo sapiens* when he is viewed against the background of the stars.

> There is nothing like astronomy to pull the stuff out of man.
> His stupid dreams and red-rooster importance: let him count
> the star-swirls.[27]

Even now that man has split the atom and is conquering space, he is still ridiculous, "and no God pities him."[28] Jeffers recalls that in his youth (he was born in 1887), it was taken for granted that the human race would last as long as the earth, but now he does not think it will work out that way; the earth will flourish long after mankind is gone. He harps on the beauty of the natural universe while dwelling with unmitigated disgust on the cruelty of the human animal. Man must break away from his self-preoccupation. If man is puffed up with delusions of grandeur, "the billion light-years cause a serene and wholesome deflation."[29]

Jeffers's Inhumanism commits him to the worship of a God who is cruel and indifferent as well as inexplicable. God in all his manifestations remains untroubled by the disasters wrought upon the earth. God is unaffected by orgasmic violence or war or the unavoidable tragedy of death. Jeffers never lets up in his jeremiads against the baneful Christian mythos. Man is not the son of God. The road Christ took plunged the world into fratricidal strife and enslaved the people to a religion of sacrifice and blood, which finds its appropriate symbolism in the cross. Robinson Jeffers, remarks one theological critic, "recognizes this scarlet threat of blood and agony that runs through all of life. For him it is the lot even of those who escape the net of life and attain to the tower beyond tragedy."[30] Jeffers confirms the fact that there is nothing after death; science demonstrates the foolishness of such mythic expectations. Once the body disintegrates in the chemistry of death, no soul survives. In conformity with his philosophy of Inhumanism, Jeffers welcomes the prospect of annihilation; death is a means of liberation. It is a difficult creed to live by. To those who cannot accept the answers he gives to the enigmas that life propounds, he replies that he cannot help himself if he writes as he does. He cannot tell lies in poetry. He cannot sing that God is love or that justice will finally prevail.

3. CONCLUSION

Jeffers, like both Schopenhauer and Nietzsche, is "religious" in his search for salvation. He would deliver man from the terrible, blind compulsion of the will. In his version of reality, human striving is futile; there is no cause for resorting to pity; as a poet he will not pander to the human craving for illusion but must reaffirm his belief that the existence or extinction of the race of man is unimportant. Those who have the power to free themselves from the dementia of sex or the opium of religion know that death is no evil. Jeffers thus dedicates his poetry to "the religion" of nihilism. He is much engrossed with the problem of determining God's nature. Though he addresses men in the language of poetry, his object is essentially a moral one: to induce men to abandon their pipe-dreams. Unlike Nietzsche, he makes no effort to transcend his nihilism. The absurd is the absolute, and the absurd is God. It is to this God that he composes a hymn of salvation.

Jeffers differs from a poet like Yeats in that he cannot praise man. He knows the truth of what Yeats declares in "The Tower":

> Death and life were not
> Till man made up the whole,
> Made lock, stock and barrel
> Out of his bitter soul,
> Aye, sun and moon and star, all,
> And further add to that
> That, being dead, we rise,
> Dream and so create
> Translunar Paradise.

He could not encourage men to dream and create the vain vision, not even within the scope of art, of a translunar paradise. Down with life! is his prevailing cry. The human infection will eventually be wiped out, mankind will die, the sun will continue to reign, the earth will resume its pristine glory. In Jeffers's view, nature, compared with the vile creature man, always comes off the victor. He consistently supports a naturalistic interpretation of existence, but when he pits man against nature it is unfailingly to the former's disadvantage. Man perverts the pure life of nature. He deludes himself into believing that he is essential to the universe whereas nature is sublimely indifferent to his existence. Jeffers's Inhumanism is rightly named: it is a nihilism that categorically denies all value to the human enterprise.[31]

Jeffers has made a memorable contribution to the cultural treasury of the race; he has kept faith with his vocation as a poet and his conception of what constitutes the truth of reality. He could not, like another artist, say to himself: "If one form of Asiatic wisdom is to teach that all is vain, and that one should be inert enough to make no effort, our Western wisdom is that knowing all to be vanity we must act to the best of our human capacity."[32] Jeffers possessed the energy but not the spirit of defiance that sustained a poet like Kazantzakis. Odysseus, Kazantzakis's hero, is willing to give himself to a cause without thought of the outcome; it is sufficient for him that he is part of the world's hidden purpose. Kazantzakis worships, like Jeffers, a God of infinite energy spiraling in space, a God of vertiginous change, who might be named "Abyss, Mystery, Absolute Darkness, Absolute Light, Matter, Spirit, Ultimate Hope, Ultimate Despair, Silence."[33] Despite his nihilism, Kazantzakis strives to remain loyal to life and his fellow men, whereas Jeffers counsels his brethren to turn away completely from humanity. For Kazantzakis, though he too suspects that mankind is the victim of a monstrous hoax which thrusts him into life and hurls him into death without his ever knowing why he was born, writing represents an act of faith. To write is to be committed. As Edwin Muir wrote in *Latitudes*, when he was still a disciple of Nietzsche: "Our first duty is to fight the idea of Happiness, to make Man tragic."[34] Jeffers fought the idea of happiness, but he could not make man tragic. Man was contemptible.

I end my study of literary perspectives with no trumpet blast of affirmation. The truth and the way have not been found. I have considered a great variety of proclaimed truths and a number of cherished illusions. I have walked along numerous winding roads of vision, none of which led to any triumphant conclusion. The mystery remains. If this leaves us very much where we began, there should be no cause for surprise. It confirms the philosophy of perspectivism that has all along been my theme. There are no privileged points of view. Man must live in uncertainty. It is the glory of literature that it saves us from a foolish dogmatism. Whether the writer regards the universe from a scientific or purely aesthetic viewpoint, he must judge it by standards that are after all human. In an ultimate sense, man cannot know the meaning of his destiny on earth, but at least he knows that he does not know. Nevertheless, he believes in the truth and cannot live without it. It is this that leads him to experiment with different perspectives and to protest against the human condition.

CONCLUSION

THE RELATIONSHIP between symbol and fact, image and event, fiction and so-called reality, is very much to the point in my dis-cussion of literary perspectives. Within a literary work the action portrayed is not real but hypothetical. The actors on the stage are not to be identified with the parts they play; the novel or drama does not consist of formal propositions to be verified as true or false but of verbal constructions which are to be judged as imaginatively true or false. Hence we cannot say explicitly what the writer has aimed at, the meaning he intended to communicate; we have but the work to guide us, the text that is the locus of all meaning. No critic, however sensitive his aesthetic response or how profound his insight, can possibly exhaust the wealth of meanings contained in a great work of literature. As Ralph Waldo Emerson says in "The American Scholar": "Each age . . . must write its own books."[1] The "poem," like reality itself, accommodates itself to a variety of interpretations. Each generation modifies the critical heritage of the past and discovers its own Shakespeare, Cervantes, and Donne. Literature thus lends itself to a multiplicity of per-spectives, which may range from a denial of reality altogether to an attempt to give a faithful representation or mimesis of reality. But whatever the vision that a literary work may incorporate, it must operate of necessity within and as a part of an existing body of conventions.

For literature is a professional discipline, a technical, highly developed art form, as well as a criticism of life. Its ontological meaning communicates itself fully and effectively only in terms of its formal structure, its unity of design, its imagery and language. Literature as art rests in ambiguity and grows out of internal tensions because the material it deals with is intractably mysterious, resistant to explicit formulation. The aesthetic meaning radiates from an existential center that is elusive, indefinable, its secret not to be grasped in any other way. How, for example, can the modern writer pretend that reality is well ordered and that life has a controlling purpose when, like Kafka, Antonin Artaud, Sartre, and Genet, he has no self that he can call his own? To apply the words of Franz Rosenzweig, a Jewish existentialist, to his case: "He is no more certain about 'I' than about the ways and purposes of the external world."[2] Or, in the words of Franz Kafka: "My doubts stand in a circle around every word."[3] This is the kind of consciousness, confused, even solipsistic, with which a number of writers in our time confront the world.

They question the ground of being but it vouchsafes no unequivocal answer, if it ventures an answer at all. They lift their voices and then, listening intently, they imagine they hear a reply. But it may be an echo. They may have imagined that they heard a sound in the forests of the night, and even if they heard it they cannot make out clearly what it means, for it is in a language that is beyond human comprehension. It is enigmatic, unfathomable, and after all their efforts to translate the mysterious message they think they received they can never be certain that there was any message at all. In visionary writing, in the work of poets like Blake, Rimbaud, Rilke, and Yeats, and in the prose writings of men like Maeterlinck, Kafka, Alain-Fournier, Julian Green, and Samuel Beckett, the mystery remains. There is no subject matter—a flower in the crannied wall, stopping by woods on a snowy evening, the song of the nightingale heard by Keats ("Was it a vision, or a waking dream?")—that is not instinct with the ineffable accents of the numinous. Under the clairvoyant gaze of the dreamer, reality disintegrates as he becomes one with the object of his contemplation. It requires no oracle of Zen Buddhism to tell us this. As Maurice Maeterlinck says: "The measure of man's greatness is the greatness of the mysteries which he cultivates or on which he dwells."[4]

The theory of symbolism is inevitably connected with a theory of knowledge. What is the relationship between object and mind, the in-itself and consciousness, the knower and that which is known? How break down the distinction between the naked "fact," the brute datum of sense, and the perceiving self? Can literature transcend this dualism between external reality and a language that functions as a mirror? The language of literature is not derived, as Chernyshevski dogmatically assumed, from an attempt to form a strict pattern of correspondence with external reality. It is in itself a creative activity. The plastic medium of imaginative language is at bottom a method of discovering the world of meaning, so that the fixed categories of "either-or," of true or false, cease to apply. The symbolic act, when closely examined, reveals the complexity of the relationship between art and life, structure and function, for the artist is driven by the need to impose meaning on the universe; he must define himself in relation to his cosmos, to his culture, and to his society. In thus endeavoring to know himself, he must strive to subdue the anarchy within himself and at the same time establish contact with "reality."

The mystery of the phenomenal universe, however, baffles all his efforts at comprehension. The mind has to create its own sense of order, but this imposed, provisional pattern offers no revelation of some transcendental reality. The mind of man cannot possibly grasp the nature of the noumenal world. Grappling with these thorny philosophical problems, the writers came to realize with Kant that it is impossible to know anything but the data furnished by the senses. It is man who, by his mental activity, provides the material out of which "order" or "unity" is established. He cannot "prove" the existence of God or uncover "the true" character of nature. What he beholds is the product of his sensory endowment, not the reflection of some vast metaphysical system. If values were somehow to be made "real," they must be projected upon the world. Man was the measure of things, the consciousness that lent reality to nature. Art makes it possible to view the world from a number of different symbolic perspectives. Literature "contemplates the absolute from the vantage point of the temporal and records the ironies and ambiguities that are the limits of the human in the face of the absolute."[5]

If the writer is convinced that reality cannot be known, if "life and the universe are incommensurable" and "no common scale any longer relates man to his physical setting,"[6] then he may be tempted to embrace illusion as representing one vital form of "the real." The sphere of reality thus becomes what the imagination makes of it. Tragedy, according to Lionel Abel, differs from metatheater in that the latter communicates more strongly the Kantian belief that "the world is a projection of human consciousness."[7] No image of the world is privileged in character. "Metatheater assumes there is no world except that created by human striving, human imagination."[8] Man, the inventor and architect of order, accepts the reality of dreams. No writer, however, feels entirely at home in a world that is phantasmagorical, the projection of fleeting shadows on the screen of consciousness. He wants to postulate a world that is enduringly real and meaningful, a world in which he can live. He cannot reconcile himself to the reality of his dreams when he knows they are but dreams. If increased scientific knowledge breaks down the old framework of religious faith, it also culminates, paradoxically, in the realization that all is illusion. Frustrated when he is confined within the limits of his metatheater, the writer continues to seek the reality behind the veil, the God in whom it would be absurd to believe because he, too, would be a personified dream.

These are some of the metaphysical conflicts which the writers of the modern age have struggled to resolve, and their creative efforts have given birth to a host of different perspectives. In this volume I have examined some of them. A literary work is dominated, I have assumed, by one or more key perspectives, as well as by a number of subordinate perspectives brought in for purposes of dramatic counterpoint. The analysis of a literary work in the light of a single perspective is not meant to imply that this perspective is a valid image of human experience or that it is free from internal contradictions. If a play is designed to show that all is illusion, then the laws of aesthetic consistency, even in the theater of the absurd, dictate that the play must be considered an exception to the rule. All is illusion except the belief that all is illusion and the play that demonstrates the universality of illusion. The play itself, in short, is no illusion. All the world's a stage except the work of the imagination which embodies this theme, unless the dramatist is prepared to argue that the audience in the theater are also actors in a play that requires them to witness a play written by another dramatist. What we get, then, as in *The Balcony* and *The Blacks,* is a play within a play within a play.

Nevertheless, the belief persists that though all is illusion, art manages to achieve some measure of "reality." Or, according to a different logical assumption, if art is of illusion all compact, then the life of society provides the true reality. Brecht, in order to destroy the theater of illusion, used the technique of alienation; he would cut off the feeling of empathy on the part of the audience so as to make them uncomfortably aware of social evils to be removed. Genet, who evinces no desire to change the world by political means, also shatters the illusion of the theater-goer that he has come to enjoy a make-believe show; gradually the spectator discovers he is witnessing the enactment of his own fantasies.

The conflict between subjectivity and objectivity, the self and the world outside it, is still with us. The writers of today are still impaled on the horns of the dilemma posed by Kantian idealism. Truth seemed unattainable. The attempt was made in some quarters to go beyond metaphysics, to base perception on the process of consciousness. The world of consciousness had to be explored, for there lay the key to the mystery of self. If phenomenology proved congenial to a number of French writers, it was because it precipitated a movement from the realm of the a priori to things themselves. Each writer is a phenomenologist in practice, even if he has never heard of the term. He deals, as he must, with things themselves, though he interprets them from a variety of perspectives.

If Salvador Dali exploits what he calls critical-paranoiac activity in his surrealist productions, he knows that the difference between him and a madman is that he is not mad. The metaphor of disease plays an important role in the fiction of Kafka and Thomas Mann, but their work—and the same is true of Dostoevski—represents a process of cure and transcendence. If the artist is neurotic, the work he creates is in effect a negation of neurosis. Life may be a thing of sound and fury, but *Macbeth* signifies "something." Each of the perspectives I have taken up in this book—the metaphor of the machine, the utopian obsession, the scientific version of reality, life as a dream or a game—discloses all sorts of complexities.

Each perspective involves a limitation since it shuts out for the time being other perspectives. Every point of view is partial and incomplete, and yet some point of view must be adopted if anything is to be said at all. As Ortega, the leading modern exponent of perspectivism, points out: "Relativism is, in the long run, scepticism and scepticism, when its justification is that it opposes all speculative theory, is in itself a theory of suicidal character."[9] But if the philosophy of perspectivism has any validity as applied to literature, then there is no definitive version of reality. Each character, in fiction or drama, lives in his own psychic universe; each work creates its own sensibility and its own vision of truth.

I have tried to trace the connection between a writer's worldview and his art, his conception of reality and the structure of his work. Does he stress the utter mysteriousness of reality like a Maeterlinck, a Rilke, a Kafka, an Alain-Fournier? Is he convinced that life is best represented in the image of a dream, a game, a nightmare, a stage? Or is he convinced that man is invested with the power to shape his world in accordance with his Promethean will? Like the rationalist in art, does he confidently assume that he knows what reality is? The great realists, according to Lukacs, placed society and its relations in the center of their fictional cosmos. For this Marxist critic, the artistic totality of a literary work "depends on the completeness of the picture it presents of the essential social factors that determine the world depicted."[10]

Literature introduces us to a number of clashing and incompatible perspectives. To the writer who believes in universal determinism, who sees the body and mind of man in the fetters of necessity, life must seem like a prison from which there is no possibility of escape. To the writer who believes in freedom of the will, however, life must often seem to resemble a game of chance. The latter image, while extremely popular, is, like the reality it purports to reflect, decidedly ambiguous. What kind of freedom is it that is exposed to hazard? Who rolls the dice, who spins the wheel? Perhaps the dice are loaded. When the chips are down, does the player ever emerge the winner? Does statistical probability govern the outcome or is the gambling house of life rigged? The tragic writers, now as in the past, furnish no definite answer to these charged questions. Frequently they resolve the conflict in an enigmatic and ironic manner. What the meaning of the pattern is, if there be a pattern at all, is left up to the reader to decide. The hero of Somerset Maugham's naturalistic novel, *Of Human Bondage*, discovers: "There was no meaning in life, and man by living served no end. It was immaterial whether he was born or not born, whether he lived or ceased to live. Life was insignificant and death without consequence."[11] Philip Carey exults in this knowledge, but the representative heroes of modern literature are usually depressed by this vision of *nada*. If there is no providence that shapes our ends, then we are to the gods as flies to wanton boys.

The philosophy of perspectivism rests on a premise that some critics condemn as not only untenable but absurd: the doctrine of relativism. Man is immersed in the flux of becoming. He is a creature of history, a victim of time, for whom this terrestrial existence is all he will ever experience. That is the only truth he can hope to know. There is no absolute; morality is relative to time and place. Change is the essence of life. New conditions give rise to new attitudes. Hence "no binding, objective, eternal values of content"[12] are acknowledged. Even God is relativized.

Perspectivism is frequently attacked on the ground that in practice an absolute relativism is impossible. Actually perspectivism, in literature, need not be hamstrung by a perverse refusal to take sides. It assumes that all points of view are equally valid. It simply underlines the limitations of language and art in the attempt to resolve all ambiguity. The writer tries to communicate what he beholds in his vision; he presents characters in action and shows how they behave under pressure, how they respond to different aspects of man's fate. Some are rebellious, others are resigned, still others invoke the name of God. Some, abject in their defeat, schizophrenically exclude the world, which they find menacing and incomprehensible. The madman, like the drug addict, prefers to dwell in his world of compensatory fantasies. The "man of affairs," "the serious man" whom Sartre accuses of bad faith, is "mad" in his own way.

If the work of art abides my question and cannot be caught on the pinhead of a definition, reality remains sphinxlike and unknowable. It is susceptible of a host of different interpretations. Each pair of eyes, as Proust maintained, views it from a uniquely situated position. The existential ambiguity persists. No single interpretation provided by the work of art is all-embracing or free from contradictions. Even when the writer strives like Jules Romains to embody a unanimist aesthetic, he is bound to leave out some aspects of human experience. In Romains's picture of the collectivity, the individual is lost. Society is the hero. By contrast, Proust's protagonists, though they frequent the salons of Paris, dwell alone, in an incommunicable solitude of the mind and heart.

Literary perspectivism, by its use of polar images, serves to make clear that the world cannot be comprehended within a rigid ideological framework; it undermines the naïve assumption that the structure of reality is reflected faithfully in the mirror of language. No perspective, not even the vaunted one of science, is sacrosanct. Scientific analogies function very much like the surprise of metaphor.

The difference seems to be that the scientific analogy is more patiently pursued, being employed to inform an entire work or movement, where the poet uses his metaphor for a glimpse only. (Yet even here we may find a similarity; the complete works of the poet show signs of a unified attitude precisely such as may be summed up in one metaphor: "He calls life a dream . . . or a pilgrimage . . . a carnival . . . or a labyrinth.")[3]

It was Nietzsche who taught the modern mind that nothing is to be believed, not even the conclusions of science. He fought against the illusion that relied on man as the measure of value. The free spirit can do without the prop of certainty, though this involved Nietzsche in a tangle of contradictions from which he could not extricate himself. If truth is a myth, then the pursuit of truth must logically be brought to an end. "The doubt of all truth is itself an act of truthfulness."[14] Nietzsche's desperate but fruitless quest for ultimate meaning led him to espouse a nihilism that cannot be borne because it cannot be lived.

In the nihilistic perspective that many post-Nietzschean writers employ, the self becomes a nonself. The antihero in Beckett's novels is transformed into a perpetual question mark, a consciousness that confronts the universe in a spirit of futile interrogation. The protagonist feels alienated and imperiled in a world which contains no hint of the divine, only the absolutism of death. All things have been rendered questionable. Modern man is not himself; he is without identity, a bundle of disparate selves. The hero as outsider is not at home in his world; his loss of self is accompanied by a corresponding loss of his sense of reality. The world outside him becomes apparitional. Self-consciousness reaches a point where thought annihilates itself; the mind is no longer under logical control. Instinct and the irrational rule the contemporary hero; dreams take possession of him; doubts assail him at every turn; the "I" that speaks and acts is a ghost in a phantasmal, surrealist landscape. All contemporary British writers, according to one critic, "sense, in one way or another, the ludicrous position of man free to act in a world in which action is difficult and insignificant. Man's position is comic, vulnerable, incongruous."[15]

The age of the modern begins with this confrontation of a world that is a paradox, a haunting mystery. The problem goes beyond the difficulty of proving that anything except sense data exists. The truth is no longer to be known. As the scientific enterprise robs men of their cultural as well as religious certitudes, as one sacred truth after another is demolished, science itself is brought up short before the barriers of the unknowable beyond which human intelligence cannot go. There is no reality except that which is refracted through the distorting lens of the human mind. In the "new" novel in France, consciousness is never sure of what it registers; the central character is never sure of his identity; the world is something to be conjectured, a dream perhaps; the truth is unknowable. Consciousness mediates the world of things, but perception is affected by the play of imagination, desire, and memory. Hence reality is glimpsed only in partial perspectives.[16] Here then is the new French novel, which portrays a world that is nonrational. The writer ceases to explain and judge the events and characters he depicts. The hero reveals himself in his monologue, his stream of consciousness, in what he does or says. This method of simply recording the flow of consciousness, without forcing it into a conceptual frame, adheres fairly closely to Husserl's phenomenology, with its assumption that the world is there but that it is perceived by consciousness. That is how the traditional dualism of outer and inner is transcended. The world in the new French novel is viewed neutrally, without the interpolation of metaphysical presuppositions. "What this means to the new novelists is the destruction of a fixed and given human nature, a personality as such, and the fragmentation of consciousness in the world."[17]

This aesthetic of fiction that aims to get rid of metaphysics confirms my point that a writer's vision of reality and his conception of the nature of man are interdependent. What man is *not* can be more or less ascertained: he is not a thing, he is not a machine, he is not merely a biological organism, an animal, a creature of instinct and conditioned reflexes. He is all these things, to be sure, but always qualitatively different, something more. He is a becoming, an active principle of transcendence, a time-binding "miracle" of nature. He is directed toward the future and can, by the concentrated force of his striving, alter the meaning of the past. He is the creator of the gods and he is godlike, too, in his distrust of these creations. He values truth more than his need for illusion. Nothing daunts him. When it becomes necessary, he sacrifices his false gods on the altars of truth. He regards even the truth with suspicion lest it become a fetish. Nothing is sacred in his eyes except this belief in the sanctity of truth. Each generation of literati behold a new truth and worship new gods.

All this may be the spindrift of illusion, a tantalizing mirage conjured up by the modern mind, but it represents more or less what man today believes he believes. He has come to a stage in his historic development where relativism prevails; even his beliefs are provisional, possibly a figment of the imagination, a vain surmise, a series of as-if fictions. He must look upon these mental constructs as if they were real, since he cannot live without them. Although baffled in his quest, knowing that life laughs at thought, he persists in his search for the truth. The modern hero may perish, but the work in which he appears, however nihilistic in content, bears witness to the greatness, though not the triumph, of the human spirit.

Relativism is in the saddle and rides mankind, or at least a goodly portion of the creative intellectuals of the Western world. My analysis of some representative specimens of our age has shown that they are predominantly concerned with the radical finitude of all being. The writers of our time have, with few exceptions, abandoned the absolute. Confined within the limits of history, man comes to realize that there are no unconditional and eternal values. This is the precarious plight of the modern hero in a world bounded on all sides by the horizons of the finite. Life in the here and now is the locus of all values; there is nothing beyond. Biological considerations are of paramount importance; the absurd conquers; opposites are united. Relativity of vision is inescapable. If there is no single standard of beauty, as Santayana pointed out long ago,[18] there is no single standard of truth or of reality.

In conclusion, it must be noted that the different literary perspectives through which life is viewed have no direct bearing on the *value* of the work produced. Despite what the Marxist critics affirm, the quality of art is not affected by the degree to which it corresponds to the nature of reality. Relativity of vision does not dispose of the question of artistic value. Kitsch is kitsch. A comic strip also adopts a point of view, and so do the didactic tracts of Horatio Alger, but these offer no serious competition to *Hamlet* or

The Adventures of Don Quixote or *The Idiot*. The universe of art is a multiverse; it is able to accommodate itself to the realism of Balzac and Flaubert, the naturalism of Zola and Dreiser, the "illusionism" of Genet, the metatheater of Pirandello, the objective hazard and psychic automatism of the surrealists, the utopianism of H. G. Wells and the antiutopianism of Aldous Huxley and George Orwell, the "religious" perspective of Graham Greene and François Mauriac, the existentialist atheism of Sartre, and the phenomenological method of the new French novelists. What it finds great difficulty in assimilating is material that is highly doctrinaire and ideological: propaganda, socialist realism, and allegory in which "the idea" is made to dominate the vision.

Art, in short, cannot be reduced to a single, all-inclusive category. The writer may, like Thomas Mann or Thomas Hardy, be influenced by Schopenhauer's pessimism, but his production must not be evaluated in terms of its abstract meaning; it is the context itself, the unique synthesis of form and content, that must be judged. Not that the novelist does not at times make use of philosophical ideas; he does, but he does not use them to propound a thesis. The function of the novelist, as novelist, is to construct a coherent universe of the imagination. In creating this universe, which constitutes his version of reality, he must of course keep faith with his own point of view, his own intuitions and insights, because no one else can tell him what is true or real.[19] Whether he assumes that art is subservient to reality or that reality is itself compounded of illusion, the work he turns out is, after all, a species of illusion, an exercise in "unreality." The drama, even when subjected to the Brechtian technique of alienation, remains drama, which is illusion.

The artist is saved from becoming the dupe of his illusions by projecting himself into a *persona*, a second voice through which he speaks. He preserves the tensions and ambiguities of life by creating other contrasting points of view. The greater the work of art—that is, the more it is under the control of the imagination—the more certain is it to provide an array of opposed or conflicting life-attitudes: life as a dream is countered by the gospel of earnest striving in the world of time. Don Quixote is balanced by the earthy Sancho Panza. The metaphor of life as a stage is offset by the effort of the characters—and their author—to break down the walls of the theater and reach out into the problematical world of reality. Though life is portrayed as a game that must be played according to the rules, the author also suggests the irrationality that presides over man's fate, the unpredictable intrusion of the absurd. Whatever perspective the writer relies upon, he is as a relativist forced to realize that art is illusion. Life remains, when all is said and done, the supreme metaphor, the incognizable mystery.

NOTES

INTRODUCTION

1. Unless otherwise specified, by point of view I do not mean the formal technique in fiction of relating experience through the angle of vision of a single narrator. Though in this book the two key terms, perspectivism and relativism, are used for the most part interchangeably, perspectivism is usually employed to refer to the writer's method, in his representation of reality, of using different points of view, none of which is accorded a privileged position. The word relativism is used in the traditional sense, as in the phrase psychological relativism or ethical relativism.

2. René Wellek, *Concepts of Criticism*, ed. Stephen G. Nichols, Jr. (New Haven: Yale University Press, 1963), p. 17.

3. Ibid., p. 20.

4. Eliseo Vivas, "Reiterations and Second Thoughts on Cultural Relativism," in Helmut Schoeck and James W. Wiggins, eds., *Relativism and the Study of Man* (Princeton: D. Van Nostrand Co., 1961), p. 61.

5. Philip Wheelwright, *Metaphor and Reality* (Bloomington: Indiana University Press, 1962), p. 6.

6. Ludwig Wittgenstein, *Tractatus Logico-Philosophicus* (New York: Harcourt, Brace & Co., 1922), 4.021.

7. Michael Polanyi, *Personal Knowledge* (Chicago: University of Chicago Press, 1958), p. 88.

8. See the section entitled "Literature and the Cultural Matrix," in Robert A. Hall, Jr., *Cultural Symbolism in Literature* (Ithaca, New York: Linguistica, 1963), pp. 9-16, an elaboration of Taine's sociological criticism emphasizing the factors of race, environment, and epoch.

9. Kenneth Burke, *A Rhetoric of Motives* (New York: Prentice-Hall, 1950), p. 198.

10. Jean-Paul Sartre, *What Is Literature?*, trans. Bernard Frechtman (New York: Philosophical Library, 1949), pp. 224-25.

11. *Novels in the Making*, ed. William E. Buckler (Boston: Houghton Mifflin Co., 1961), p. 215.

12. Bernard C. Heyl distinguishes between subjectivism and relativism, rejecting the former as vague and riddled with internal contradictions. See his discussion of "Relativism" in *New Bearings in Esthetics and Art Criticism* (New Haven: Yale University Press, 1957), pp. 125-55.

13. Leo Spitzer, *Linguistics and Literary History* (New York: Russell & Russell, 1962), p. 41.

14. "*Qua* moralist, Cervantes is not at all 'perspectivistic.' " Ibid., p. 73.

15. Emerson R. Marks, *Relativist and Absolutist* (New Brunswick: Rutgers University Press, 1955), p. 25.

16. "The collapse of the rationalist notion of time leaves the current theory of time irrationally culturally relativistic; and the irrational relativism of time is connected with the irrational relativism of human needs." Norman O. Brown, *Life against Death* (Middletown, Connecticut: Wesleyan University Press, 1959), p. 273.

17. Arthur Koestler, *The Act of Creation* (New York: Macmillan Co., 1964), p. 183.

18. Erich Fromm, D. T. Suzuki, and Richard De Martino, *Zen Buddhism and Psychoanalysis* (New York: Harper & Brothers, 1960), p. 10.

19. Martin Esslin, *The Theatre of the Absurd* (Garden City, New York: Doubleday & Co., 1961), p. 86.

20. See Wylie Sypher, *Rococo to Cubism in Art and Literature* (New York: Random House, 1960), p. 287.

21. Georg Lukacs, *The Historical Novel*, trans. Hannah and Stanley Mitchell (London: Merlin Press, 1962), p. 91.

22. *Documents of Modern Literary Realism*, ed. George J. Becker (Princeton: Princeton University Press, 1963), p. 36.

23. Georg Lukacs, *Studies in European Realism*, trans. Edith Bone (London: Hillway Publishing Co., 1960), p. 13.

24. Leo Lowenthal insists that even these individual or private experiences are part of the social matrix. "The social meanings of this inner life of the individual are related to the central problems of social change."

Leo Lowenthal, *Literature, Popular Culture, and Society* (Englewood Cliffs, New Jersey: Prentice-Hall, 1961), p. xv.

25. Julian Marias, *Reason and Life*, trans. Kenneth S. Reid and Edward Sarmiento (New Haven: Yale University Press, 1956), p. 212.

26. See Heinz Politzer, *Franz Kafka* (Ithaca, New York: Cornell University Press, 1962).

27. One French scholar, Gaston Bachelard, has written a series of studies examining literature according to the way it makes use of the four elements: air, water, fire, and earth. (See Eva M. Kushner, "The Critical Method of Gaston Bachelard," in Bernice Slote, ed., *Myth and Symbol* [Lincoln: University of Nebraska Press, 1963], pp. 39-50.)

28. Friedrich Nietzsche, *Joyful Wisdom*, trans. Thomas Common (New York: Frederick Ungar Publishing Co., 1960), pp. 340-41.

29. For an analysis of the profound difference between the Orient and the Occident in their world-view, see Wilhelm Worringer, *Abstraction and Empathy*, trans. Michael Bullock (London: Routledge & Kegan Paul, 1953), p. 16.

30. André Malraux, *The Temptation of the West*, trans. Robert Hollander (New York: Vintage Books, 1961), pp. 97-98.

31. Ibid., p. 118.

32. See Martin Johnson, *Time and Universe for the Scientific Conscience* (Cambridge: University Press, 1952), pp. 24-27 passim.

33. Herbert Fingarette, *The Self in Transformation* (New York and London: Basic Books, 1963), p. 232.

CHAPTER 1

1. William E. Harkins, *Karel Capek* (New York: Columbia University Press, 1962), p. 102.

2. H. Vaihinger, *The Philosophy of 'As If'*, trans. C. K. Ogden (New York: Harcourt, Brace & Co., 1925), p. xli.

3. Ibid., p. xlvii.

4. Ibid., p. 46.

5. Ibid., p. 106.

6. Ibid., p. 306.

7. Jules de Gaultier, *From Kant to Nietzsche*, trans. Gerald M. Spring (New York: Philosophical Library, 1961), p. 23.

8. Max Scheler, *Man's Place in Nature*, trans. Hans Meyerhoff (Boston: Beacon Press, 1961), p. xii.

9. M. Merleau-Ponty, *Phenomenology of Perception*, trans. Colin Smith (London: Routledge & Kegan Paul, 1962), p. xix.

10. Everett W. Knight, *Literature Considered as Philosophy* (London: Routledge & Kegan Paul, 1957), p. 31.

11. Joshua C. Taylor, *Futurism* (New York: Museum of Modern Art, 1961), p. 124.

12. Hyatt Howe Waggoner, *The Heel of Elohim* (Norman: University of Oklahoma Press, 1950), p. 138.

13. *Documents of Modern Literary Realism*, ed. George J. Becker (Princeton: Princeton University Press, 1963), p. 94.

14. For a brief discussion of how Newtonian mechanics is replaced by Einsteinian relativity in fiction, see Charles I. Glicksberg, *Literature and Religion* (Dallas, Texas: Southern Methodist University Press, 1960), p. 193; and, by the same author, "The Relativity of the Self," in *The Self in Modern Literature* (University Park: Pennsylvania State University Press, 1963), pp. 71-95.

15. Bertrand Russell, *Human Knowledge* (New York: Simon & Schuster, 1948), p. 290.

16. "We are the victims of the Demon of the Absolute, the Deluder who can take many forms, but who for us appears as the idol of Nature set high on the throne of omnipotence." Paul Elmer More, *The Demon of the Absolute*, New Shelburne Essays (Princeton: Princeton University Press, 1928), 1:x-xi.

17. Ibid., 1:40.

18. Lawrence Durrell, *A Key to Modern British Poetry* (Norman: University of Oklahoma Press, 1952), p. 26.

19. Jack Lindsay, *Death of the Hero* (London: Studio Books, 1960), p. 173.

20. Ibid., pp. 173-74.

21. "To my mind the *relativity of God* denotes a point of view which ceases to regard God as an 'absolute', *i.e.* removed from the human subject and existing outside all human conditions, but as, in a certain sense, dependent upon the human subject." C. G. Jung, *Psychological Types*, trans. H. Godwin Baynes (New York: Harcourt, Brace & Co., 1926), p. 300.

22. Aldous Huxley, *Do What You Will* (New York: Doubleday, 1929), p. 267.

23. Ibid., p. 316.

24. Aldous Huxley, *Ends and Means* (New York: Harper & Brothers, 1937), p. 312.

25. Aldous Huxley, *Point Counter Point* (New York: Modern Library, 1928), p. 228.

26. Ibid.

27. Ibid.

28. Ibid., p. 293.

29. Ibid., p. 349.

30. Ibid., p. 350.

31. D. H. Lawrence, *Psychoanalysis and the Unconscious and Fantasia of the Unconscious* (New York: Viking Press, 1960), p. 208.

32. Ibid., p. 209.

33. Max Frisch, *The Chinese Wall*, trans. James L. Rosenberg (New York: Hill & Wang, 1961), p. 46.

34. James Gindin, *Postwar British Fiction* (Berkeley and Los Angeles: University of California Press, 1962), p. 9.

CHAPTER 2

1. See Richard Samuel and R. Hinton Thomas, *Expressionism in German Life, Literature, and the Theatre* (Cambridge, England: W. Heffer & Sons, 1939), p. 59.

2. See Robert Gibson, *The Quest of Alain-Fournier* (New Haven: Yale University Press, 1954).

3. As Havelock Ellis says in his introduction: "It was by his 'dream' that Fournier was led, and that dream . . . was at once the reality of the past and the desire of the future." Alain-Fournier, *The Wanderer*, trans. Françoise Delisle (Boston: Houghton Mifflin Co., 1928), p. xxxii.

4. Robert Champigny, *Portrait of a Symbolist Hero* (Bloomington: Indiana University Press, 1954), p. 109.

5. Marcel Proust, *The Past Recaptured*, in *Remembrance of Things Past*, trans. C. K. Scott Moncrieff and Frederick A. Blossom (New York: Random House, 1932), 2:1013.

6. Marcel Proust, *Cities of the Plain*, in ibid., 2:272.

7. Ibid., p. 293.

8. Marcel Proust, *The Captive*, in ibid., p. 512.

9. Ibid., p. 559.

10. Roger Shattuck, *Proust's Binoculars* (New York: Random House, 1963), p. 44.

11. Maurice Maeterlinck, *The Intruder*, trans. Richard Hovey (New York: Dodd, Mead & Co., 1911), p. 26.

12. Ibid., p. 39.

13. Ibid, p. 44.

14. Ibid., p. 76.

15. Ibid.

16. Ibid., p. 87.

17. Ibid., p. 88.

18. Maurice Maeterlinck, *Our Eternity*, trans. Alexander Teixeira de Mattos (New York: Dodd, Mead & Co., 1914), p. 12.

19. Ibid., p. 42.

20. W. D. Halls, *Maurice Maeterlinck* (Oxford: Clarendon Press, 1960), p. 172.

21. Alexander Kaun, *Leonid Andreyev* (New York: B. W. Huebsch, 1924), p. 106.

CHAPTER 3

1. René Laforgue, *The Relativity of Reality*, trans. Anne Jouard (New York: Nervous and Mental Disease Monographs, 1940), pp. 85-88 passim.

2. See Charles I. Glicksberg, "The Psychology of Surrealism," *Polemic*, no. 8, pp. 46-55.

3. Anna Balakian, *Surrealism* (New York: Noonday Press, 1958), p. 154.

4. Louis Aragon, "The Return to Reality," *International Literature*, no. 1 (1936), p. 104.

5. Yves Duplessis, *Surrealism*, trans. Paul Capon (New York: Walker & Co., 1962), p. 34.

6. Ibid., pp. 100-101.

7. D. H. Lawrence, *Psychoanalysis and the Unconscious and Fantasia of the Unconscious* (New York: Viking Press, 1960), p. 5.

8. See Charles I. Glicksberg, "D. H. Lawrence: The Prophet of Surrealism," *The Nineteenth Century* 144 (1948): 229-37.

9. Charles I. Glicksberg, "The Madness of Salvador Dali," *New Mexico Quarterly* 17 (1947): 424.

10. C. G. Jung, *The Development of Personality* (London: Routledge, 1954), p. 115. Quoted in Alex Comfort, *Darwin and the Naked Lady* (London: Routledge & Kegan Paul, 1961), p. 51.

11. See Charles I. Glicksberg, "Literature and Freudianism," *Prairie Schooner* 23 (1949): 370-71; Lionel Trilling, "Art and Neurosis," in *The Liberal Imagination* (New York: Viking Press, 1950), pp. 160-80; and Frederick J. Hoffman, *Freudianism and the Literary Mind* (New York: Grove Press, 1959), pp. 1-58 passim.

12. See Charles I. Glicksberg, "Art and Disease," *The Nineteenth Century* 145 (1949): 180-88.

13. Thomas Mann, *Freud, Goethe, Wagner*, trans. T. H. Lowe-Porter (New York: Alfred A. Knopf, 1937), p. 42.

14. Thomas Mann, *Stories of Three Decades*, trans. T. H. Lowe-Porter (New York: Alfred A. Knopf, 1951), p. 414.

15. Ibid., p. 99.

16. Ibid., p. 100.

17. Ibid., p. 103.

18. Ibid., p. 108.

19. Ibid.

20. Ibid., p. 128.

21. D. H. Lawrence, *Selected Literary Criticism*, ed. Anthony Beal (New York: Viking Press, 1956), p. 265.

22. Herman J. Weigand, *Thomas Mann's Novel Der Zauberberg* (New York and London: D. Appleton-Century Co., 1933), p. 98.

23. *Short Novels of the Masters,* ed. Charles Neider (New York: Rinehart & Co., 1948), p. 148.

24. Antonin Artaud, *The Theater and Its Double,* trans. Mary Caroline Richards (New York: Grove Press, 1958), p. 148.

25. See Carl Solomon, "Report from the Asylum," in Gene Feldman and Max Gartenberg, eds., *The Beat Generation and the Angry Young Men* (New York: Dell Publishing Co., 1958), pp. 171-82; also "Madness; The Theme of Unreason," in Lawrence Lipton, *The Holy Barbarians* (New York: Julian Messner, 1959), pp. 156-70.

26. Lionel Trilling remarks that "an ambivalent attitude toward Freudianism is perhaps inevitable and may be even healthy." Lionel Trilling, *Freud and the Crisis of Our Culture* (Boston: Beacon Press, 1955), p. 42.

CHAPTER 4

1. One stimulating book in this field is Erving Goffman, *The Presentation of Self in Everyday Life* (Garden City, New York: Doubleday & Co., 1959).

2. René Marill-Albérès, *Jean-Paul Sartre,* trans. Wade Baskin (New York: Philosophical Library, 1961), pp. 70-71.

3. J. Huizinga, *Homo Ludens* (Boston: Beacon Press, 1955), p. 3.

4. Henrik Ibsen, *Three Plays,* trans. Una Ellis-Fermor (Harmondsworth, Middlesex: Penguin Books, 1957), p. 244.

5. Lawrence Thomas, *André Gide* (London: Secker & Warburg, 1950), p. 249.

6. Franz Kafka, *The Penal Colony,* trans. Willa and Edwin Muir (New York: Schocken Books, 1948), p. 255.

7. Huizinga, *Homo Ludens,* p. 212.

8. Luigi Pirandello, *To Clothe the Naked and Two Other Plays,* trans. William Murray (New York: E. P. Dutton & Co., 1962), p. 91.

9. Ibid., p. 91.

10. Ibid.

11. Ibid., p. 68.

12. Hermann Hesse, *Magister Ludi,* trans. Mervyn Savill (New York: Frederick Ungar Publishing Co., 1949), p. 17.

13. Ibid., p. 40.

14. Ibid., p. 76.

15. Ibid., pp. 76-77.

16. Ibid., p. 353.

17. Ibid., pp. 360-61.

18. Elizabeth Sewell, *The Field of Nonsense* (London: Chatto & Windus, 1952), p. 114.

19. Lewis Carroll, *Logical Nonsense,* ed. Philip C. Blackburn and Lionel White (New York: G. P. Putnam's Sons, 1934), p. 176.

20. Roger Caillois, *Man, Play, and Games*, trans. Meyer Barash (New York: Free Press of Glencoe, 1961), p. 7.

21. Arthur Adamov, *Ping-Pong*, trans. Richard Howard (New York: Grove Press, 1959), p. 11.

22. Ibid., p. 48.

23. Ibid., p. 66.

24. Ibid., p. 126.

25. Ibid.

26. Ibid., p. 128.

27. Ibid., p. 129.

28. Ibid.

CHAPTER 5

1. *Collected Works of V. I. Lenin*, vol. 13: *Materialism and Empirico-Criticism*, trans. David Kvitko (New York: International Publishers, 1927), p. 300.

2. Leon Livingstone, "Ortega y Gasset's Philosophy of Art," *Publications of the Modern Language Association* 67 (1952): 615.

3. Allardyce Nicoll, *The World of Harlequin* (Cambridge: University Press, 1963), p. 25.

4. Jean-Paul Sartre, *The Devil and the Good Lord and Two Other Plays*, trans. Kitty Black (New York: Alfred A. Knopf, 1960), p. 167.

5. Ibid., p. 174.

6. Ibid., p. 225.

7. Ibid., p. 256.

8. "Most relationships are based on some partial depersonalizing tendency in so far as one treats the other not in terms of any awareness of who or what he might be in himself but as virtually an android robot playing a role in a large machine in which one too may be acting yet another part." R. D. Laing, "Ontological Insecurity," in Hendrik M. Ruitenbeek, ed., *Psychoanalysis and Existential Philosophy* (New York: E. P. Dutton & Co., 1962), p. 51.

9. George Kateb, *Utopia and Its Enemies* (New York: Free Press of Glencoe, 1963), p. 161.

10. Quoted in Elizabeth Sewell, *The Human Metaphor* (Notre Dame: University of Notre Dame Press, 1964), p. 118.

11. Albert Camus, *Notebooks, 1935-1942*, trans. Philip Thody (New York: Alfred A. Knopf, 1963), p. 63.

12. Ibid., p. 64.

13. George T. Wright, *The Poet in the Poem* (Berkeley and Los Angeles: University of California Press, 1960), pp. 18-19.

14. *The Autobiography of William Butler Yeats* (New York: Macmillan Co., 1938), p. 183.

15. See "Dance and Soul," in Paul Valéry, *Dialogues*, trans. William McCausland Stewart (New York: Pantheon Books, 1956), p. 52.

16. Walter H. Sokel, ed., *Anthology of German Expressionist Drama* (Garden City, New York: Doubleday & Co., 1963), p. 10.

17. For a discussion of the mask in the primitive world, see Joseph Campbell, *The Masks of God* (New York: Viking Press, 1959), p. 21. For a fascinating study of the employment of the mask in Japan, see Seiroka Noma, *Masks*, English adaptation by Meredith Weatherby (Rutland, Vermont, and Tokyo, Japan: Charles E. Tuttle Co., 1957). For an admirable discussion of the use of the mask in its magical, religious, and then theatrical role, see Kenneth MacGowan and Herman Rosse, *Masks and Demons* (New York: Harcourt, Brace & Co., 1923).

18. Lionel Abel, *Metatheatre* (New York: Hill & Wang, 1963), p. 79.

19. See Robert J. Nelson, *Play within a Play* (New Haven: Yale University Press, 1958).

20. For this distinction I am indebted to Joseph E. McMahon, *The Imagination of Jean Genet* (New Haven: Yale University Press, 1963), p. 160.

21. See the essay, "Concerning Sincerity," in which Rivière discusses the complex meaning of sincerity toward the self. Jacques Rivière, *The Ideal Reader*, trans. Blanche A. Price (New York: Meridian Books, 1960), p. 76. For a scholarly treatment of the quest for sincerity in French literature, see Henri Peyre, *Literature and Sincerity* (New Haven: Yale University Press, 1963).

22. Jean Genet, *The Maids*, trans. Bernard Frechtman (New York: Grove Press, 1954), p. 8.

23. Ibid., p. 16.

24. Jean Genet, *The Balcony*, trans. Bernard Frechtman (New York: Grove Press, 1958), p. 4.

25. Ibid., p. 17.

26. Ibid., p. 27.

27. Ibid., p. 30.

28. Ibid., p. 32.

29. Ibid., p. 33.

30. Ibid., p. 115.

31. Jean Genet, *The Blacks*, trans. Bernard Frechtman (New York: Grove Press, 1960), p. 3.

32. Ibid., p. 4.

33. Norman Mailer, in "The White Negro," has resuscitated the myth of the Negro's extraordinary sexual power. This, he insists, is no myth. "Sexuality is the armature of Negro life. Without sexuality they would've perished." Norman Mailer, *The Presidential Papers* (New York: G. P. Putnam's Sons, 1963), p. 147. He comes closer to Genet's position when

he maintains that this is what the average white man actually thinks of the Negro's sexual prowess.

34. Genet, *The Blacks*, p. 12.

35. Ibid., p. 23.

36. Ibid., p. 24.

37. See the chapter, "As We Saw Them—As They See Us," in Julius E. Lips, *The Savage Hits Back* (New Haven: Yale University Press, 1937), pp. 29-59. For Ralph Ellison's symbolic treatment of the color motif in his novel, *Invisible Man*, see Charles I. Glicksberg, "The Symbolism of Vision," *Southwest Review* 39 (1954): 256-65.

38. Genet, *The Blacks*, p. 39.

39. Ibid., p. 106.

40. Ibid., pp. 114-15.

41. Ibid., p. 126.

CHAPTER 6

1. *Mayakovsky and His Poetry*, compiled by Herbert Marshall (London: Transatlantic, 1945), p. 36.

2. Ibid., p. 61.

3. See V. G. Belinsky, *Selected Philosophical Works* (Moscow: Foreign Languages Publishing House, 1948).

4. N. G. Chernyshevski, "Essays on Gogol Period in Russian Literature," in *Selected Philosophical Essays* (Moscow: Foreign Languages Publishing House, 1953), p. 489.

5. Ibid., p. 394. Like Chernyshevski, Belinsky felt unlimited enthusiasm for the mighty potentialities of the scientific method. "To hell with metaphysics: that word signifies the supernatural, consequently, the nonsensical." Belinsky, *Philosophical Works*, p. 493.

6. N. G. Chernyshevski, *What Is to Be Done?* trans. Benjamin R. Tucker, revised and abridged by Ludmila R. Turkevich (New York: Vintage Books, 1961), p. 12.

7. Ibid., p. 114.

8. Ibid., p. 259.

9. See David Magarshack, *Dostoevsky* (New York: Harcourt, Brace & World, 1962), p. 234.

10. Rufus W. Mathewson, Jr., *The Positive Hero in Russian Literature* (New York: Columbia University Press, 1958), p. 117.

11. Georg Lukacs, *Studies in European Realism*, trans. Edith Bone (London: Hillway Publishing Co., 1950), p. 111.

12. Ibid., pp. 224-25.

13. Vera Alexandrova, *A History of Soviet Literature*, trans. Mirra Ginsburg (Garden City, New York: Doubleday & Company, 1963), p. 354.

14. See Bernice Slote, ed., *Literature and Society* (Lincoln: University of Nebraska Press, 1964).

15. Eugenia W. Herbert, *The Artist and Social Reform* (New Haven: Yale University Press, 1961), p. 87.

16. Erich Fromm defines alienation as "essentially experiencing the world and oneself passively, receptively, as the subject separated from the object." Erich Fromm, *Marx's Concept of Man* (New York: Frederick Ungar Publishing Co., 1961), p. 44.

17. Lukacs, *European Realism*, p. 2.

18. Ibid., p. 4.

19. Raymond A. Bauer, *The New Man in Soviet Psychology* (Cambridge: Harvard University Press, 1952), p. 5.

20. *Brecht on Theatre*, ed. John Willett (New York: Hill & Wang, 1964), p. 180.

21. John Willett, *The Theatre of Bertold Brecht* (London: Methuen & Co., 1959), p. 77.

22. In order to correct the misconceptions that have been spread about Brecht's work, Eric Bentley half-seriously defines epic theater as lyric theater. Eric Bentley, "Epic Theater Is Lyric Theater," in Leroy R. Shaw, ed., *The German Theater Today* (Austin: University of Texas Press, 1963), p. 91.

23. *Brecht on Theatre*, p. 193.

24. Ibid., p. 196.

25. Baal symbolizes the Phoenician idol of fertility; the cult of Baal exemplifies what might be called the typical Dionysiac orgies.

26. Bertold Brecht, *Baal*, trans. Eric Bentley and Martin Esslin, in Walter H. Sokel, ed., *Anthology of German Expressionist Drama* (Garden City, New York: Doubleday & Co., 1963), p. 340.

27. Ibid., p. 350.

28. Ibid., p. 360.

29. Bertold Brecht, *Seven Plays*, ed. Eric Bentley (New York: Grove Press, 1961), p. 38.

30. Ibid., p. 47.

31. Ibid., p. 61.

32. Ibid., p. 64.

33. Ibid., p. 155.

34. Ibid., p. 251.

35. Walter H. Sokel, "Brecht's Split Characters and His Sense of the Tragic," in Peter Demetz, ed., *Brecht* (Englewood Cliffs, New Jersey: Prentice-Hall, 1962), p. 133.

36. *The Measures Taken*, English version by Eric Bentley, in Eric Bentley, ed., *The Modern Theatre* (Garden City, New York: Doubleday & Co., 1960), pp. 258-59.

37. Ibid., p. 261.

38. Ibid.

39. Ibid., pp. 261-62.

40. Ibid., p. 270.

41. Ibid., p. 276.

42. Ibid., p. 277.

43. Ibid., p. 278.

44. Ibid., p. 281.

45. Demetz, *Brecht*, p. 109.

46. Eugene Ionesco, *Notes and Counter Notes*, trans. Donald Watson (New York: Grove Press, 1964), p. 135.

47. Raymond Williams, *The Long Revolution* (New York: Columbia University Press, 1961), p. 278.

CHAPTER 7

1. See J. L. Talmon, "The Decline of Messianism?," in Raymond Aron, ed., *World Technology and Human Destiny* (Ann Arbor: University of Michigan Press, 1963), p. 164.

2. Ibid., p. 166.

3. See Morse Peckham, *Beyond the Tragic Vision* (New York: George Braziller, 1962), p. 197.

4. See W. H. G. Armytage, *Heavens Below* (Toronto: University of Toronto Press, 1961), p. 63.

5. H. G. Wells, *The War of the Worlds, The Time Machine, and Selected Short Stories* (New York: Platt & Munk, 1963), p. 380.

6. Bernard Bergonzi, *The Early H. G. Wells* (Manchester: University Press, 1961), p. 22.

7. Ibid., p. 131.

8. Richard Gerber, *Utopian Fantasy* (London: Routledge & Kegan Paul, 1955), p. 67.

9. Bergonzi, *H. G. Wells*, p. 173.

10. H. G. Wells, *A Modern Utopia* (London: Thomas Nelson & Sons, n. d.), p. 102.

11. H. G. Wells, *The Idea of a World Encyclopedia* (London: L. & V. Woolf, 1936), p. 5.

12. Ibid., p. 21.

13. Wells, *Modern Utopia*, p. 354.

14. Arnold Toynbee, *A Study of History* (London: Oxford University Press, 1949), 6:97.

15. The material in this section is an expanded and revised version of the article by Charles I. Glicksberg, "Anti-Utopianism in Modern Literature," which appeared in the Summer 1952 issue of the *Southwest Review*.

16. It is this psychological insight which led Hawthorne to put these words into the mouth of Coverdale, the narrator of the story in *The*

Blithesdale Romance. The latter acknowledges that it is "wiser, if not more sagacious, to follow out one's day-dream to its natural consummation, although, if the vision have been worth the having, it is certain never to be consummated otherwise than by a failure. And what of that? Its airiest fragments, impalpable as they may be, will possess a value that lurks not in the most ponderous realities of any practicable scheme." *The Complete Novels and Selected Tales of Nathaniel Hawthorne* (New York: Modern Library, 1937), p. 444.

17. Kurt W. Marek, *Yestermorrow*, trans. Ralph Manheim (New York: Alfred A. Knopf, 1961), p. 12.

18. Ibid., p. 13.

19. Martin Buber, *Paths in Utopia*, trans. R. F. C. Hull (New York: Macmillan, 1950), pp. 5-6.

20. Ibid., p. 129.

21. Ibid., p. 132.

22. Leon Trotsky, *Literature and Revolution* (New York: Russell & Russell, 1957), p. 252.

23. Ibid., p. 255.

24. Irving Howe, *A World More Attractive* (New York: Horizon Press, 1963), p. 217.

25. Aldous Huxley, *Brave New World* and *Brave New World Revisited* (New York: Harper & Brothers, 1960), p. xix.

26. See Aldous Huxley, *The Perennial Philosophy* (New York: Harper & Brothers, 1945), pp. 294-301.

27. Aldous Huxley, *Ape and Essence* (New York: Harper & Brothers, 1948), pp. 51-52.

28. Arthur Koestler also contends that the eruption of the irrational was caused by the work of the scientist. Arthur Koestler, *The Yogi and the Commissar* (New York: Macmillan Co., 1945), p. 12.

29. Arthur Koestler, *The Age of Longing* (New York: Macmillan Co., 1951), p. 136.

30. J. D. Bernal, *The Social Function of Science* (New York: Macmillan Co., 1939), p. 382.

31. George Kateb, *Utopia and Its Enemies* (New York: Free Press of Glencoe, 1963), p. 8.

32. Since the time of the Renaissance, the utopian imagination has been drawn to this Promethean myth. For Bacon, in *New Atlantis*, the end sought is "the knowledge of causes, and secret motions of things; and the enlarging of the bounds of human empire, to the effecting of all things possible." *Famous Utopias of the Renaissance* (New York: Hendricks House and Farrar, Straus, 1948), p. 240.

33. B. F. Skinner, *Walden Two* (New York: Macmillan Co., 1962), p. 103.

34. Ibid., p. 105.

35. Ibid., p. 162.

36. Scientific utopianism, like communism, is uncompromisingly atheistic. Western civilization has triumphed without the concept of God, and this means "that Christianity is dead." (Marek, *Yestermorrow*, p. 74.) Technology drives out not only the Christian God but all the gods of other lands which adopt Western forms of civilization.

37. Skinner, *Walden Two*, p. 229.

38. Ibid., p. 239.

39. Ibid., p. 256.

40. Ibid., p. 257.

41. Ibid., p. 273.

42. Ibid., p. 290.

43. Ibid., p. 308.

44. Floyd W. Matson condemns Skinner's science of society as "an altogether explicit disavowal of the freedom and responsibility, as well as the moral and political primacy, of the human person." Floyd W. Matson, *The Broken Image* (New York: George Braziller, 1964), p. 80. For an equally hostile critique of *Walden Two*, see Joseph Wood Krutch, *The Measure of Man* (New York: Grosset & Dunlap, 1954), p. 90.

45. Kateb, *Utopia*, p. 176.

CHAPTER 8

1. Floyd W. Matson, *The Broken Image* (New York: George Braziller, 1964), p. viii.

2. J. P. Stern, *Ernst Jünger* (New Haven: Yale University Press, 1953), p. 45.

3. Wylie Sypher, *Loss of the Self in Modern Literature and Art* (New York: Random House, 1962), p. 15.

4. See Isaiah Berlin, *Historical Inevitability* (London and New York: Oxford University Press, 1955), p. 22.

5. Raymond Aron, ed., *World Technology and Human Destiny* (Ann Arbor: University of Michigan Press, 1963), p. 66.

6. *New York Times*, January 1, 1962.

7. James T. Culbertson, *The Minds of Robots* (Urbana: University of Illinois Press, 1963), p. 59.

8. See Ruthven Todd, *Tracks in the Snow* (New York: Charles Scribner's Sons, 1947), pp. 21-22.

9. Joseph Needham, *Man a Machine* (New York: W. W. Norton & Co., 1928), pp. 66-67.

10. Ibid., pp. 95-96.

11. Murray Turbayne, *The Myth of Metaphor* (New Haven: Yale University Press, 1962), p. 3.

12. A. S. Eddington, *The Nature of the Physical World* (New York: Macmillan Co., 1946), p. 282.

13. Georg Kaiser, *Gas (I)*, trans. Herman Scheffauer (New York: Frederick Ungar Publishing Co., 1957), p. 76.

14. Ibid., p. 96.

15. See the play, "Tempo," by Nikolai Pogodin, which carries to an absurd degree the Russian romanticization of technology, in Eugene Lyons, ed., *Six Soviet Plays* (Boston: Houghton Mifflin Co., 1934).

16. William E. Harkins, *Karel Capek* (New York: Columbia University Press, 1962), p. 60.

17. Ibid., p. 91.

18. Max Frisch, *The Chinese Wall*, trans. James L. Rosenberg (New York: Hill & Wang, 1961), p. 25.

19. Ibid., p. 25.

20. Ibid., p. 28.

21. Ibid., p. 47.

22. Ibid., p. 48.

23. Ibid., p. 49.

24. Ibid., p. 97.

25. Ibid., p. 108.

26. Karl Jaspers, *The Future of Mankind*, trans. E. B. Ashton (Chicago: University of Chicago Press, 1961), p. 4.

CHAPTER 9

1. R. D. Laing, "Ontological Insecurity," in Hendrik M. Ruitenbeek, ed., *Psychoanalysis and Existential Philosophy* (New York: E. P. Dutton & Co., 1962), p. 50.

2. Lawrence Durrell, *A Key to Modern British Poetry* (Norman: University of Oklahoma Press, 1952), p. 21.

3. Aldous Huxley, *Literature and Science* (New York: Harper & Row, 1963), p. 59.

4. See Joseph Wood Krutch, *The Modern Temper* (New York: Harcourt, Brace, 1929), for a searching analysis of the impact of science on the creative imagination of modern man.

5. Quoted in David Magarshack, *Dostoevsky* (New York: Harcourt, Brace & World, 1962), p. 353.

6. Alfred J. Ayer, *Language, Truth and Logic* (New York: Oxford University Press, 1936), p. 161.

7. Ibid., p. 170.

8. René Laforgue, *The Relativity of Reality*, trans. Anne Jouard (New York: Nervous and Mental Disease Monographs, 1940), p. 59. Despite Laforgue's emphasis on the relativity of truth and reality, psychoanalysis does draw a fundamental distinction between what it calls illusion or wishful thinking and the *reality* principle.

9. Friedrich Nietzsche, *Joyful Wisdom*, trans. Thomas Common (New York: Frederick Ungar Publishing Co., 1960), pp. 277-78.

10. Ibid., p. 279.

11. Albert William Levi, *Literature, Philosophy and the Imagination* (Bloomington: Indiana University Press, 1962), p. 47.

12. See Charles I. Glicksberg, "D. H. Lawrence and Science," *Scientific Monthly* 63 (1951): 99.

13. D. H. Lawrence, *Apocalypse* (New York: Viking Press, 1932), p. 43.

14. Ibid., pp. 44-45.

15. M. Chaning-Pearce, *The Terrible Crystal* (New York: Oxford University Press, 1941), p. 187.

16. William York Tindall, *D. H. Lawrence and Susan His Cow* (New York: Columbia University Press, 1939), p. 31.

17. Aldous Huxley, ed., *The Letters of D. H. Lawrence* (New York: Viking Press, 1932), p. 96.

18. D. H. Lawrence, *Phoenix*, ed. E. D. McDonald (New York: Viking Press, 1936), p. 535.

19. D. H. Lawrence, *Selected Literary Criticism*, ed. Anthony Beal (New York: Viking Press, 1956), p. 106.

20. C. P. Snow, *The Two Cultures and the Scientific Revolution* (Cambridge: University Press, 1959), p. 14.

21. Norbert Wiener, *The Human Use of Human Beings* (Boston: Houghton Mifflin Co., 1950), p. 26.

CHAPTER 10

1. Ernst Cassirer, *The Philosophy of Symbolic Forms*, trans. Ralph Manheim (New Haven: Yale University Press, 1955), 2:40.

2. Leonard Forster, *Poetry of Significant Nonsense* (Cambridge: University Press, 1962), pp. 28-31.

3. Ernst Cassirer, *Language and Myth*, trans. Suzanne K. Langer (New York: Harper & Brothers, 1946), p. 11.

4. Mark Schorer, *William Blake* (New York: Holt, 1946), p. 39.

5. G. M. Kirkwood, *A Study of Sophoclean Drama* (Ithaca, New York: Cornell University Press, 1958), pp. 27-28.

6. D. H. Lawrence, *Apocalypse* (New York: Viking Press, 1932), p. 45.

7. Wylie Sypher, *Rococo to Cubism in Art and Literature* (New York: Random House, 1960), p. 6.

8. Mircea Eliade, *Myths, Dreams, and Mysteries*, trans. Philip Mairet (London: Harvill Press, 1960), p. 16.

9. Friedrich Nietzsche, *The Birth of Tragedy* and *The Genealogy of Morals*, trans. Francis Golffing (Garden City, New York: Doubleday & Co., 1956), p. 137.

10. Hugo von Hofmannsthal, *Selected Prose*, trans. Mary Hottinger,

Tania Stern, and James Stern (New York: Pantheon Books, 1952), p. xxvi.

11. Paul Ginestier, *The Poet and the Machine*, trans. Martin B. Friedman (Chapel Hill: University of North Carolina Press, 1961), p. 10.

12. D. H. Lawrence, *Psychoanalysis and the Unconscious and Fantasia of the Unconscious* (New York: Viking Press, 1960), p. 112.

13. Hans Kelsen, *Society and Nature* (Chicago: University of Chicago Press, 1943), p. 23.

14. Aldous Huxley, ed., *The Letters of D. H. Lawrence* (New York: Viking Press, 1932), p. 291.

15. Ibid., p. 366.

16. Ibid., p. 693.

17. Ibid.

18. Lawrence, *Apocalypse*, p. 31.

19. An excellent discussion of Lawrence and how he coped with the problem of alienation is to be found in Philip Rieff, "A Modern Mythmaker," in Henry A. Murray, ed., *Myth and Mythmaking* (New York: George Braziller, 1960), pp. 240-75.

20. D. H. Lawrence, *The Rainbow* (New York: Modern Library, 1915), pp. 416-17.

21. D. H. Lawrence, *Women in Love* (New York: Modern Library, 1920), p. 47.

22. Ibid., p. 545.

23. Harry T. Moore, ed., *D. H. Lawrence's Letters to Bertrand Russell* (New York: Gotham Book Mart, 1948), p. 63.

24. *Letters of D. H. Lawrence*, p. 613.

25. D. H. Lawrence, *The Plumed Serpent* (New York: Vintage Books, 1955), p. 60.

26. Ibid., p. 78.

27. Ibid.

28. Ibid., p. 315.

29. Ibid., p. 372.

30. Ibid., p. 394.

31. George Orwell, "Inside the Whale," *New Directions in Prose and Poetry* (Norfolk, Conn.: New Directions, 1940), p. 222.

32. D. H. Lawrence, *Selected Literary Criticism*, ed. Anthony Beal (New York: Viking Press, 1956), p. 156.

33. Ibid., p. 158.

34. Lawrence, *Apocalypse*, p. 200. *Apocalypse* has had a considerable effect on the literature of our time, especially in the rise of the New Apocalypse, a movement dedicated, among other things, to the pursuit of myth and dream to make possible the emergence of the whole man. See also Karl Shapiro, Bernice Slote, and James E. Miller, Jr., *Start with the Sun* (Lincoln: University of Nebraska Press, 1963).

CHAPTER 11

1. Leo Spitzer, "Language of Poetry," in Ruth Nanda Anshen, ed., *Language: An Enquiry into Its Meaning and Function* (New York: Harper & Brothers, 1957), p. 231.

2. Ronald Duncan, Kenneth Jupp, and Bernard Kops, *Satan, Socialites, and Solly Gold* (New York: Coward-McCann, 1961), p. 105.

3. H. Vaihinger, *The Philosophy of 'As If'*, trans. C. K. Ogden (New York: Harcourt, Brace & Co., 1925), pp. 162-63.

4. See Hans Jaeger, "Heidegger's Existential Philosophy and Modern German Literature," *Publications of the Modern Language Association* 67 (1952): 655-83.

5. Hugo von Hofmannsthal, *Selected Prose*, trans. Mary Hottinger, Tania Stern, James Stern (New York: Pantheon Books, 1952), p. 133.

6. See Robert Emmet Jones, *The Alienated Hero in Modern French Drama* (Athens, Georgia: University of Georgia Press, 1962). See also Victor Brombert, *The Intellectual Hero* (Philadelphia: J. B. Lippincott Co., 1961).

7. George Wellwarth, *The Theater of Protest and Paradox* (New York: New York University Press, 1964), p. 32.

8. See Mercedes Monjian, *Robinson Jeffers: A Study in Inhumanism* (Pittsburgh: University of Pittsburgh Press, 1958).

9. Robinson Jeffers, *Roan Stallion, Tamar, and Other Poems* (New York: Modern Library, 1953), p. 282.

10. According to one critic, Christ for Jeffers "is the emblem of man's utopian compulsions, the utmost love for humanity." Radcliffe Squires, *The Loyalties of Robinson Jeffers* (Ann Arbor: University of Michigan Press, 1956), p. 123.

11. Robinson Jeffers, *Dear Judas and Other Poems* (New York: Horace Liveright, 1929), p. 17.

12. Ibid.

13. Jeffers, *Roan Stallion*, p. 54.

14. Robinson Jeffers, *Cawdor and Other Poems* (New York: Horace Liveright, 1928), p. 157.

15. Ibid., p. 158.

16. Robinson Jeffers, *The Double Axe and Other Poems* (New York: Random House, 1948), p. vii.

17. Ibid., p. 21.

18. Ibid., p. 53.

19. Ibid., p. 72.

20. Ibid., p. 81.

21. Ibid., p. 93.

22. Ibid., p. 105.

23. Robinson Jeffers, *Hungerfield and Other Poems* (New York: Random House, 1954), p. 5.

24. Ibid., p. 95.

25. Ibid.

26. Ibid.

27. Robinson Jeffers, *The Beginning and the End and Other Poems* (New York: Random House, 1963), p. 18.

28. Ibid., p. 19.

29. Ibid., p. 71.

30. Amos N. Wilder, *Theology and Modern Literature* (Cambridge: Harvard University Press, 1958), p. 110.

31. Carpenter questions whether Jeffers's philosophy is actually nihilistic in character. If his philosophy "merely excluded man from nature, and if it denied all value and nobility to man, it would be . . . nihilistic." Frederic I. Carpenter, *Robinson Jeffers* (New York: Twayne Publishers, 1962), p. 118.

32. Amédée Ozenfant, *Foundations of Modern Art*, trans. John Rodker (New York: Dover Publications, 1952), p. 231.

33. Nikos Kazantzakis, *The Saviors of God*, trans. Kimon Friar (New York: Simon & Schuster, 1960), p. 101.

34. Edwin Muir, *Latitudes* (New York: B. W. Huebsch, 1926), p. 238.

CONCLUSION

1. Stephen E. Whicher, ed., *Selections from Ralph Waldo Emerson* (Boston: Houghton Mifflin Co., 1957), p. 67.

2. Franz Rosenzweig, *Understanding the Sick and the Healthy* (New York: Noonday Press, 1953), p. 33.

3. Joseph Kersh, trans., and Max Brod, ed., *The Diaries of Franz Kafka: 1910-1913* (New York: Schocken Books, 1948), p. 32.

4. Maurice Maeterlinck, *Our Eternity*, trans. Alexander Teixeira de Mattos (New York: Dodd, Mead & Co., 1914), p. 31.

5. Frederick J. Hoffman, "Form and Circumstances," in *Approaches to the Study of Twentieth-Century Literature* (East Lansing: Michigan State University Press, 1961), p. 9.

6. René Huyghe, *Art and the Spirit of Man* (New York: Harry N. Abrams, 1962), p. 459.

7. Lionel Abel, *Metatheatre* (New York: Hill & Wang, 1963), p. 113.

8. Ibid., p. 113.

9. José Ortega y Gasset, *The Modern Theme*, trans. James Cleugh (New York: Harper & Brothers, 1961), p. 20.

10. Georg Lukacs, *Studies in European Realism*, trans. Edith Bone (London: Hillway Publishing Co., 1950), p. 147.

11. Somerset Maugham, *Of Human Bondage* (New York: George H. Doran Co., 1915), p. 559.

12. J. Von Rintelen, *Beyond Existentialism*, trans. Hilda Graef (London: George Allen & Unwin, 1961), p. 65.

13. Kenneth Burke, *Permanence and Change* (New York: New Republic, 1935), p. 127.

14. Karl Jaspers, *Nietzsche and Christianity*, trans. E. B. Ashton (Hinsdale, Illinois: Henry Regnery Co., 1961), p. 82.

15. James Gindin, *Postwar British Fiction* (Berkeley and Los Angeles: University of California Press, 1962), p. 236.

16. See Laurent Le Sage, *The French New Novel* (University Park: Pennsylvania State University Press, 1962).

17. Ibid., p. 17.

18. George Santayana, *The Sense of Beauty* (New York: Charles Scribner's Sons, 1936), p. 99. First published in 1896.

19. See "Toward a Concept of Existentialist Literature," in Eugene F. Kaelin, *An Existentialist Aesthetic* (Madison: University of Wisconsin Press, 1962), pp. 386-404.